W9-DBA-238

WHO IS
BASEBALL'S
GREATEST
HITTER?

WHO IS BASEBALL'S GREATEST HITTER?

REVISED AND UPDATED

JEFF KISSELOFF

HENRY HOLT AND COMPANY
NEW YORK

For Marie, Amanda, and Zach, my new family—
and not a .200 hitter in the bunch

Henry Holt and Company, LLC
Publishers since 1866
115 West 18th Street
New York, New York 10011

Henry Holt is a registered
trademark of Henry Holt and Company, LLC

Published in Canada by Fitzhenry & Whiteside Ltd.,
195 Allstate Parkway, Markham, Ontario L3R 4T8.

Library of Congress Cataloging-in-Publication Data
Kisseloff, Jeff.
Who is baseball's greatest hitter? / by Jeff Kisseloff.
p. cm.
Includes index.
Summary: Statistics, stories, and historical details help the reader to decide
which baseball player is the greatest hitter ever.
1. Baseball players—Rating of—Juvenile literature. 2. Batting (Baseball)—
Juvenile literature. [1. Baseball players. 2. Baseball—History.] I. Title.
GV865.A1 K55 2000 796.357'092'2—dc21 [B] 99-44495

ISBN 0-8050-6733-7 / First revised and updated paperback edition, 2001

First published in hardcover in 2000 by Henry Holt and Company
Revised and updated paperback edition published in 2001

Printed in the United States of America
on acid-free paper. ∞

1 3 5 7 9 10 8 6 4 2

Photo credits: Courtesy of the Atlanta Braves: p. 3; courtesy of
the San Francisco Giants: pp. 7, 72, 99; courtesy of the Pittsburgh
Pirates: p. 15; courtesy of the New York Yankees: pp. 25, 32, 68,
84; courtesy of the National Baseball Hall of Fame Library,
Cooperstown, New York: pp. 29, 37, 48, 52, 55, 65, 80, 94; courtesy of the Seattle Mariners: p. 41; courtesy of the San Diego
Padres: p. 44; courtesy of the St. Louis Cardinals: p. 76; courtesy of the Chicago White Sox: p. 101; courtesy of the Boston
Red Sox: p. 111.

CONTENTS

LET'S TALK HITTING

A guy spots a buddy sitting on a park bench. Perched next to his friend is a dog. The fellow says, "This is Rover. He's the smartest dog in the world. He talks."

"No way."

"Yup. Listen, I'll ask him a question. Rover, who hit 60 home runs in a season in 1927?"

The dog barks, "Roof, roof."

"See?" his owner says proudly. "He said Babe Ruth. Pretty amazing, huh?"

"That's ridiculous," says his friend.

"No, it isn't," insists the owner. "Listen, I'll ask him another."

He looks at his dog. "Rover, who was the first player to hit 700 homers in his career?"

"Roof, roof," says the dog.

"See, I told you he can speak."

"C'mon, he's just barking," says his friend. "I'll tell you what, let me ask him a question."

"Okay."

The friend thinks for a second. "Okay, Rover, answer this. Who hit .367 for his career and was called the greatest hitter who ever lived?"

The dog goes, "Roof, roof."

The friend says with disgust, "See? Everyone knows the answer isn't Babe Ruth. Your dog can't talk."

The dog's ears perk up. Suddenly it says, "Or was it Ty Cobb?"

This book will try to answer the same question the dog was pondering: who is baseball's greatest hitter? But at the same time it will teach you about statistics and how to judge and weigh their value.

Along the way, it will explore the game's wonderful history. No sport has a past as rich as baseball's. Just look at the colorful nicknames of some of the game's greatest players: the Babe, the Georgia Peach, Joltin' Joe, Dizzy, Big Six, the Big Train, the Big Hurt. And name a sport with more miracles, like the Miracle Braves of '14, the Miracle of Coogan's Bluff in '51, and the Miracle Mets of 1969.

Statistics are a big part of baseball's tradition. Say 367 to a baseball fan, and like the dog the person should answer, "Ty Cobb's lifetime batting average." How about 755? "Hank Aaron's home runs." Now, of course, there's 70 for Mark McGwire's incredible 1998 season and 66 for Sammy Sosa's brilliant run at the title.

Those are just some of the numbers that every serious baseball fan carries in his or her head, like Cy Young's 511 career victories, Nolan Ryan's seven no-hitters, and Joe DiMaggio's 56-game hitting streak. And here's another one—2,632, the number of consecutive games played by Cal Ripken, Jr.

Debating what those numbers mean is as much a part of baseball's tradition as the seventh-inning stretch. It even has a name: the hot stove league, because in the old days during the winter when farmers didn't have much to do, they would gather round the stove and talk baseball.

It's no different today. Everybody has an opinion about which was the greatest team and who was the best centerfielder or the smartest manager. Those arguments are often based on statistics. By the time you finish reading this book, you'll know many of baseball's most important statistics, and you'll be able to join in those conversations with some thoughts of your own.

The question our hot stove league will be debating is who is the greatest hitter in baseball history. But this book isn't only about numbers. The statistics are gateways to hundreds of stories about the players and the games that have made baseball the national pastime.

For example, Ty Cobb's lifetime batting average tells you he must have rapped out a lot of hits. But read further. You'll learn how he got some of them by sharpening his cleats like knifepoints before every game to terrorize opposing infielders when he would slide into a base.

Ted Williams was the last man to hit over .400. But there's a story that goes along with it that you will read about in the section on the Splendid Splinter. It tells you much more about him than his batting average does.

In that way, statistics are more than just numbers, and this book is about more than just baseball. It's about comparing, something you do every day whether you realize it or not.

Let's say your mother wants you to ride your bike to the store to pick up a loaf of bread. On the shelf are two loaves of whole wheat. One is homemade, and the other is a brand name. You love whole wheat bread with your peanut butter and jelly. Which one will you buy? They both cost the same, but maybe one has ten more slices. Which is worth more? Sounds easy. But wait. Maybe the one that has fewer slices tastes better. On the other hand, maybe the one that normally tastes better is three days older, so it's not as fresh as the other. So which will it be? You'll have to weigh the different factors and make your decision.

As you decide on the best hitter in baseball history, your skills at comparison shopping will be tested in much the same way. Maybe two hitters have the same average. Maybe one hit more home runs; maybe the other drove in more runs. But maybe he played with better players. Is it any wonder that Lou Gehrig had so many runs batted in? Look who was hitting in front of him—Babe Ruth with his .342 lifetime average.

The point is there is more than meets the eye. That goes for when you are weighing players, bread, grades in school, cars, presidents, anything really that involves comparing two or more items. Sometimes, a single statistic can tell us all kinds of different things, and other times, it will tell us very little. That one loaf may give you more but it may not be tastier.

Let's take a famous baseball statistic: 61. That's the number of home runs that Roger Maris hit in 1961, setting the major league record for homers in a season. It topped Ruth's old record by one and stood until Mark McGwire pounded it in 1998.

So until Big Mac came along, Maris was the game's greatest home run hitter. Let's look at a few more numbers. Ruth hit 714 home runs over his career; Maris hit 275. Here's something else:

Ruth hit his 60 home runs in a 154-game season. In 1961, the major league season was 162 games. So was Maris a better home run hitter than Ruth? Hardly. But he had some season in 1961, didn't he? And it wasn't easy. The story goes that as Maris approached Ruth's record, the pressure on him became so intense that his hair began to fall out.

Ruth didn't have that kind of pressure. When he hit 61, he beat his own record of 59. He set that record in 1921. You know who was second in 1921? Bob Meusel. With 24! That's how dominating Ruth was.

So who do you think is the best hitter who ever lived? How about today's big heroes, like McGwire, Ken Griffey, Jr., Barry Bonds, Frank Thomas, or Tony Gwynn? What about yesterday's giants like Big Ed Delahanty, Sam Thompson, or Tris Speaker? Or who was that guy on the Cardinals your grandfather is always talking about, Stan Musial? There was also Honus Wagner, Rogers Hornsby, and George Sisler. Never heard of them? You will have after you read this book.

Each of the following chapters features a single player. And each argues why this player should be considered among the best. At the end of each chapter is a small section called "The Rundown." In it, "Hits" summarizes the arguments about what makes the player so great, while "Outs" suggests why the player may not have been the best.

To make things easier, we have already pared the list down. Players like Ducky Medwick, Pete Rose, Reggie Jackson, Mike Piazza were (or are) all terrific hitters. You can make a strong case to include each of them in this book, but in one way or another they weren't quite as stellar as the other players already included. Do you disagree? That's fine, because in the end, it's up to you to weigh the information and decide. If you think there's a solid case for Rose or Piazza, make it. We've included all 32 players' important lifetime statistics, so you can do some additional figuring for yourself. Maybe you will find a new angle to clinch your argument.

How the Game Has Changed

Comparing numbers when it comes to baseball players is more complicated than you think. That's because the game has changed so much over the years. If it wasn't for the diamond and nine players on the field, you might not recognize a baseball game from the 1870s or 1890s if it was played today. Back then pitchers could take a running start before throwing home, and they couldn't raise their arms above their shoulders. Also, the batter could tell the pitcher where he wanted the ball, high or low.

Fielders played with mitts that were barely larger than today's winter gloves, and they played on fields that were as rough as the neighborhood schoolyard. There would be a rope strung across the outfield, and fans (called "cranks" then) would stand behind it and watch the game. If a player happened to hit a ball into the roped area, the outfielder would have to chase it. Of course, if the outfielder was on the visiting team, the crowd was not going to help him find the ball. Sometimes they even hid it!

Since that period, many rule changes and new strategies and techniques have continued to change the game. Even today, the game is different from the way it was 20 or 30 years ago. Thirty years from now, people will look back at the early 2000s and say how old-fashioned it was.

Here are just some of the early rules changes. They are important to keep in mind when comparing players of different eras.

1879—The pitcher's box is reduced from six feet to four.

1880—A walk is eight balls.

1881—The pitching distance is increased from 45 feet to 50.

1881—Seven balls make a walk.

1881—An out can no longer be recorded by catching a foul on one bounce.

1883—The release point for the pitcher is as high as his shoulder, not higher.

1884—The restrictions on pitching style are lifted, but the pitcher can take only one step before delivery.

1886—Six balls are a walk.

1887—Five balls are a walk.

1887—For one season, a base on balls counts as a hit.

1887—The batter can no longer call for a high or a low pitch.

1889—The pitching box is replaced by a 12 inch × 4 inch slab.

1889—A walk is now four balls.

1893—The pitching distance is moved back to 60 feet 6 inches.

1901—Up to two fouls are counted as strikes in the National League. (Before then they didn't count as strikes.)

1903—Up to two fouls are counted as strikes in the American League.

Hitting Marshmallows

Around the year 1900 began what has since been called "the Dead Ball era" because the game was played with a ball that had a hard rubber core and a soft cover and couldn't be hit very far. The umpires only had a few balls to put into play. If one was hit into the stands, the usher would attempt (with only some success) to take it away from the fan who caught it.

As the ball got batted around during a game, its cover would get softer and softer. By the ninth inning it was as soft as a marshmallow. And if you have ever tried to hit a marshmallow, you know they don't travel very far.

The ball would also become filthy—deliberately as pitchers and fielders rubbed all sorts of things into it (talcum powder was a favorite) to make it unhittable. By the late innings, the ball was nearly black, and in a time when games were played in parks with no lights, the ball would be hard to follow as it came out of the pitcher's hand. This helped make home runs as rare as snow in July, so few players tried. Mostly, they just looked to get on base and move the runner ahead by placing ground balls or smacking line drives past the infielders. That's what made the game of the Dead Ball era mostly a scientific one. One team tried to outthink—not overpower—the other side.

A player who went for home runs was looked at the same way as someone who brushed his teeth once a week. The popular *Spalding Baseball Guide* called home run hitters selfish, a "rutty class of batsmen." It said a home run was "one of the least difficult hits as it needs only muscle and not brains to make it."

Babe Ball

Baseball changed dramatically in the 1920s. They called it "the lively ball era" for good reason. Led by the phenomenal Babe Ruth, batting and slugging averages shot up after 1920.

Ruth popularized the idea that games could be won with one swing of the bat. Suddenly, runs were being scored in bunches. From 1910 to 1919, the American League scored an average of 4,751 runs a season. From 1920 to 1929, it scored an average of 6,038 runs a season. That's a huge jump.

There were several reasons for this. Many people have suggested a livelier ball was put in play after 1920, but the baseball makers said it wasn't true. They said the ball was the same as it had always been. But pitchers said no. They claimed the seams were sewed differently. The new ball had a flatter stitching, they said. That made it much more difficult to grip and to control a curveball. Because of that, they had to throw more fastballs, which made it much easier for hitters to time the pitches.

Maybe they were right, maybe not. But there's no disputing that there were more balls put into play. That happened because in 1920 a pitcher named Carl Mays killed Ray Chapman with a pitched ball. Chapman may not have seen the ball because it was so discolored. After that, the owners ruled that once a ball became discolored it was to be replaced. When the ball became more visible, it also became more hittable.

In 1920, most pitchers lost one of their biggest weapons—the spitball, which dipped sharply when it reached the plate. The pitch was outlawed except for those pitchers who were known to use it most of the time. They were allowed to continue to throw it until they retired. Here's a good trivia question: who threw the last legal spitball? The answer is Burleigh Grimes in 1934.

Rise, Fall, Rise, Fall

Averages continued to rise through the early 1930s. Then they dipped down in the '40s after the players returned from World War II. Again, there were many reasons for this. In 1950, the strike zone was lowered to below the knees, making it easier for pitchers to throw strikes.

You also had a new kind of pitcher throwing those strikes. There were relief specialists before, but managers began using them differently and more effectively in the late 1940s. Before, a relief pitcher was a washed-up starter who was no longer very capable. In 1950 a reliever named Jim Konstanty, who led the

Phillies to the National League crown, even won the MVP award. Joe Black, Joe Page, and Hoyt Wilhelm were all relievers and were stars.

This meant that a starting pitcher wasn't expected to complete every game. Now, he could throw harder, knowing that when he ran out of gas there was a strong backup in the bullpen whose only job was to complete the game.

To give you an idea of how the game changed, the number of saves recorded by relief pitchers in 1957 was 196. The league's earned run average (ERA) that year was 3.79. In 1927, relief pitchers recorded 115 saves, and the league ERA was 4.13. That year, American League pitchers recorded 585 complete games. In 1957, the number was 354. That means when Babe Ruth hit 60 home runs in 1927, he faced a lot more tired pitchers in the late innings than a hitter would in 1957.

Pitchers also developed new pitches. The most prominent was the slider, which was introduced in the mid-1920s but wasn't widely used until after World War II. The slider looks like a fastball but, like the spitball, dips at the plate.

Another change that resulted in lower averages was night baseball. The first night game—here we go with another trivia answer—was played in Cincinnati in 1935. By the late '40s, night baseball was in full swing, and players found that hitting under the lights was harder to do.

Night games also played havoc with their sleep. Before, when games were all played in the afternoon, there was always plenty of time to rest before the next one. Now, a team might have a day game after a night game. Suddenly, you had a lot of tired hitters taking their swings.

From the 1960s to Today

Starting in the early '60s the major leagues began to expand from 16 teams to the present 30. That also cost the players much needed nap time. In the old days, they would go by train to a city, spend three or four days, and then travel to another city. That gave them lots of rest, and the traveling wasn't hard. Now, not only do they play day games after night games, but a night game in Los Angeles might be followed by a day game in New York.

As the league expanded, teams began moving out of their old-fashioned parks into new ones. Many of the new stadiums such as Pittsburgh's Three Rivers or Oakland's Alameda County Stadium were round, which meant they had huge swaths of foul territory. That made for more outs. It was also getting easier to catch the ball because gloves were getting larger and larger. They got so big they prompted Casey Stengel to complain, "They're not gloves; they're appliances."

Then in the '70s came another new pitch, the split-fingered fastball, which was thrown even harder than a slider and had a much bigger drop as it crossed the plate. All of these factors helped squash the high averages.

But gradually, the pendulum began to swing the other way until today when the hitters seem to have the advantage.

This phase began in the late '60s, when the pitching mound was lowered and the strike zone was made smaller. Expansion thinned out the pitching talent. Pitchers who might normally be in the minor leagues are now starting for major league teams because there is simply not enough pitching talent to go around. As a result, earned run averages are skyrocketing.

At the same time, new ballparks, such as Baltimore's Camden Yards and Jacob's Field in Cleveland, are getting smaller again, so more home runs are being hit.

The arrival of artificial turf in the mid-1960s also changed the game dramatically. Ground balls that were previously outs were skipping by infielders for hits, and hard-hit singles in the outfield were suddenly going for doubles and triples.

Highlight Reel

Today's players have access to videotape. Teams invest thousands of dollars in taping systems and readily supply their players with tape, because it allows them to study opposing pitchers and also to look carefully at their own swings to spot mistakes they might be making.

Umpires have also cut down on the strike zone to the point where it seems to be the size of a postcard. And although no one is commenting officially, some observers claim that baseballs have been wound tighter in recent years. That makes them travel farther when they are smashed by the likes of a Mark McGwire or Ken Griffey, Jr.

Another factor helping today's hitters is conditioning. We simply know more about keeping the body healthy for a longer period of time than people did back when Babe Ruth was playing. In the 1920s and '30s, a player who was 32 or 33 was often considered over-the-hill. Now, due to things like weight training and better nutrition, it is not unusual for a player to still be near the top of his game when he is in his middle or even late thirties.

But advances in science work both ways. In the middle of the 1998 season, a controversy surrounding McGwire pointed up another development that has made hitters stronger—literally. This involves food supplements that several players including Big Mac admitted to using or drugs such as steroids or human growth hormones that some may take but won't admit to because they are illegal. Both the steroids and the food supplements make the players stronger, but while the evidence regarding any bad health effects caused by the supplements is not clear, scientists do know that steroids can cause serious damage to the body. In 1999, McGwire said he stopped taking the supplement, and he still hit home runs.

Adding It All Up

All the rules changes in the world are not going to make a bad hitter into Babe Ruth. Ted Williams talks about five basic ingredients a player needs in order to become a great hitter. The first is intelligence. Then there is courage, eyesight, power, and timing. He adds that "only a very select few make full use of them throughout their careers."

To find out who did, Williams suggests you look at the numbers, and that's precisely what we're going to do.

Here are some of the most important statistics that will help you choose:
    • Lifetime batting average: You get this by taking the player's number of hits and dividing it by the number of at bats. For example, if a player has 40 hits in 100 at bats, you would divide 40 by 100 and see that the player's average is .400.

Does having the highest average necessarily make the player the best hitter? Maybe, maybe not. You already know about Ty Cobb owning the highest lifetime average, but Rogers Hornsby had the best five years in a row when he hit .397, .401, .384, .424, and .403 from 1921 to 1925. How much does that count?

• Home runs: Who had the most? That's one way of looking at it. Who had the most for each time at bat? That's another way. Right now, Mark McGwire has the best average with a four-bagger for every 10.628 times at bat. Babe Ruth is second with one for every 11.76 times at bat. Hank Aaron slammed one in every 16.38 at bats, but so far he has hit more home runs than anybody.

Ralph Kiner, who played in the '40s and '50s mostly for Pittsburgh and the Cubs, didn't hit as many lifetime home runs as Aaron, but he hit a home run in every 14.1 at bats and led the National League in round-trippers for seven straight years. That's a record, so where does that put him? He is now an announcer for the New York Mets. He is famous for saying, "Home run hitters drive Cadillacs; singles hitters drive Fords." What he is saying of course is that the big money goes to the guys who hit the long ball because that's what is most important. Of course nowadays when a third-string shortstop can earn over a million a year, any major leaguer can afford a Cadillac—and a Ford.

One player not on the list is Josh Gibson. He supposedly hit some 962 home runs over the course of his career. He also was the only person ever to hit a fair ball out of Yankee Stadium. But he didn't hit one home run in the major leagues. That's because he played before blacks were allowed in the majors. But he was so good, those who saw him play called him "The Black Babe Ruth."

None of the players who starred in what were called the Negro Leagues are included in this book. That's not because they don't deserve to be. Anyone who compiles a list of the game's greatest hitters who doesn't include the likes of Gibson, Oscar Charleston, Cool Papa Bell, Judy Johnson, and Buck Leonard ought to have his or her head examined. But this is a book based on statistics, and Negro League statistics were never accurately compiled. It's a shame because there will never be a full record of how great those players were. In a way, the white players lose as well, because only a complete record of all who played the game, black and white, can allow us to fully evaluate and appreciate their talent.

• Hits: Ty Cobb held the record for most hits in a career until he was passed by Pete Rose. Does that make Rose a better hitter? Rose had 65 more hits than Cobb, but he also had over 2,500 more at bats. That's reflected in his lifetime batting average. At .303, it's 64 points lower than Cobb's.

Cobb and Rose had a lot in common. Both were willing to do whatever it took on the field to win. Even when a pitcher walked him, Rose would run to first. Other players thought he was showing them up, so they gave him the nickname "Charlie Hustle."

But Rose and Cobb were very different in another way. Cobb hated blacks. On several occasions, he started fights with them and hurt them so badly they ended up in the hospital. When Rose came up, he played so hard all the time that other players on his team didn't like him. The only ones who did were the few black players on the team, who also felt left out. The veteran black players took Rose under their wings and showed him how to be a major leaguer. Some of the white players didn't like that and gave Rose a hard time, but Rose didn't care what color his friends were.

• Total bases: You get this number by adding up the total number of bases a player has reached from walks, errors, singles, doubles, triples, and homers. You can make an argument that the person with the most total bases in his career is the best hitter.

Hank Aaron is the lifetime leader in total bases with 6,856. That's a lot, especially when you consider no one really knew what to make of Aaron when he first came up with the Braves in 1954. He was quiet and not very big, but everyone noticed his quick wrists. While most home run hitters were big men with great power in their legs and arms, Aaron got his strength from his bat speed. Aaron was a very consistent player. He hit between 20 and 45 home runs for 20 straight years. He was so dangerous at the plate that other teams would allow him to bunt for hits. Once Aaron asked Jackie Robinson about this, and Robinson replied, "We'll give you first base anytime you want."

• Runs scored: The team that scores the most runs wins, so the great hitters scored a lot of runs. But what if you were a great hitter on an awful team? Wouldn't that affect how many runs you scored during your career?

In the Dead Ball era scores of 1–0 and 2–1 were common, so there were great hitters in that period who didn't score a lot of runs. For them, you have to take other factors into account.

• Runs batted in: Great hitters drive in a lot of runs, or do they? Let's remember the Dead Ball era again. In 1908, Ty Cobb led the American League with 108 RBIs. In second place was his teammate Sam Crawford with 80. In 1998, Juan Gonzalez had over 100 RBIs by the All-Star break. Does that make him a better hitter than Cobb?

Minnie Minoso didn't play in the Dead Ball era, but he might as well have. He played for the 1950s "Go-Go" White Sox. They weren't very good hitters, but they won a lot of games because of their excellent pitching and defense. Minoso, though, was a terrific hitter. He batted .298 for his career with some good RBI seasons, but imagine how many RBIs he would have had playing on a team like the Yankees, which had stellar hitters, including Mickey Mantle and Yogi Berra, from the top to the bottom of their lineup.

One thing Minoso did do was play a long time. This guy just refused to get old. He actually played in five different decades, the '40s, '50s, '60s, '70s, and '80s, when he made two appearances at the plate in 1980 at the age of 58. He came to the plate twice and didn't get a hit, but who cares. Can you imagine your grandfather taking his swings against major league pitching?

• Slugging percentage: This is an interesting number. It's the percentage of extra-base hits for each at bat. You get the slugging percentage by adding up the player's total bases and dividing it by the player's at bats. The higher the number, the more productive the hitter. Ask yourself this: Tris Speaker batted .344 over the course of his career. Ralph Kiner hit .279. But Kiner's slugging percentage was .548. Speaker's was .500. Who was more valuable?

• Titles: Maybe it's impossible to compare players from the 1900s with those who are playing today. Let's think of another way of doing it. How about comparing how each one was in his own era? How many batting titles did Ty Cobb win compared to Tony Gwynn? How many home run titles did Babe Ruth win as compared to Ken Griffey, Jr.? What does that tell you? Well, basically it tells you who was the best of his era.

So, who is the greatest hitter of any era? Let's find out.

WHO IS BASEBALL'S GREATEST HITTER?

Hank Aaron.

HANK AARON

Nickname: Hammerin' Hank
Given name: Henry Louis Aaron
Born: February 5, 1934, Mobile, Alabama
Size: 6' 180 lbs.
Bats: right
Throws: right
Position: rightfield, DH
Career: 1954–1976

Hank Aaron was a skinny 18-year-old shortstop for the Kansas City Clowns of the Negro Leagues when he was signed by the Milwaukee Braves. Nobody thought he would even hit 300 home runs in the majors. Forget about Babe Ruth's mark of 714. Most fans thought that was unbreakable by anyone. But there he was in 1974, circling the bases for the 715th time. He was on his way to 755 home runs. Now, people say that record will never be broken.

How did he do it? With the quickest wrists in the business, that's how. "Trying to sneak a pitch past Hank Aaron is like trying to sneak the sunrise past a rooster," said Curt Simmons, who pitched against Aaron in the 1950s and '60s. Aaron was not the big man that Ruth or Jimmie Foxx was, but he more than made up for it with his bat speed. He didn't hit tape-measure home runs like Mickey Mantle, but a home run counts the same whether it goes 565 feet or 365 feet, just as long as it clears the fence.

What Hammerin' Hank did was smash line drives, screaming ones that were hit so hard pitchers were afraid of him when he came up to the plate in his deceptively easy gait. The reliever Tug McGraw was asked the best way to pitch to Aaron, and he said, "The same way as to anybody else, except don't let go."

Aaron was a great clutch hitter. He holds the major league record for career runs batted in with 2,297. An excellent season for RBIs is anything higher than 100. Aaron knocked in more than 100 runs in a season 11 times. That's a National League record. Another important stat is the number of runs a player scores in a season. Again, 100 runs is considered excellent. Aaron topped 100 runs 15 times. That's a major league record.

But let's face it, when you go to the ballpark, you want to see someone hit the ball over the fence. And when you choose up sides for a game, don't you almost always pick the guy who can hit the big one for you when the game is on the line?

No one was as consistent at it as Aaron was. He slugged 30 or more home runs in a season 15 times. He had his best year as a slugger when he was 37 years old in 1971. That year, he smashed 47 homers, had 118 RBIs, and led the league in slugging with .669.

What did Aaron think was the key to his success? Work. "I've always had a little ability," he said, "but I always work at my weakness and study opposing pitchers."

And think about this. Unlike Ruth, Aaron was a right-handed hitter. More than three fourths of the pitchers he faced were right-handed. That put him at a real disadvantage at the plate, because it is easier to see a pitch if it is not coming right at you, but he still managed to hit all those home runs. No wonder he once said if he could do it all over again he would have been a switch-hitter. Imagine how many homers he would have hit then!

Maybe even more important than the number of home runs he hit was how Aaron handled the pressure as he approached Babe Ruth's lifetime record. Many people didn't want him to pass the Babe. Aaron received mounds of hate mail. Some of the writers even threatened his life if he continued to press on toward the record. In the clubhouse were hundreds of reporters. They all wanted to talk to him. "I don't want them to forget Babe Ruth," he told them over and over again. "I just want them to remember me."

They will.

More Numbers

- Aaron led the league in total bases eight times, a major league record.
- He had more than 300 total bases in a season 15 times, another major league record.
- He holds the following records:
  - Home runs (755)
  - Extra-base hits (1,477)
  - Total bases (6,856)
  - RBIs (2,297)
- Aaron is also third in hits (3,771), third in games (3,298), third in runs scored (2,174), and second in at bats (12,364).
- He is the first player to have 3,000 hits and 500 home runs.
- He established 19 records during his career.
- He made the All-Star team every year he was in the majors—24 times.
- Aaron won two batting titles.
- He was the MVP only once, but he was in the top 10 among MVP votes 12 times.

The Rundown

HITS: Aaron was all about consistency. If you were looking for a hitter who was great year in and year out, he was your man. He owns several of the most important lifetime batting records, including one of the greatest of all—the lifetime home run mark. Until Aaron came along, most baseball experts thought that record was unbreakable. While it is true that many of his records stem from the fact that he simply played a long time, when he did play he was always regarded as among the very best, maybe even the best.

OUTS: He didn't set nearly as many single-season records. He never hit 50 home runs in a season. He only led the league in homers, slugging, and RBIs four times each. In contrast, Babe Ruth led the league in slugging 13 times, in homers 12 times, and he lost four seasons as a regular because he was pitching. Otherwise, Ruth's numbers might have been even higher.

Barry Bonds.

BARRY BONDS

Given name: Barry Lamar Bonds
Born: July 24, 1964, Riverside, California
Size: 6′2″ 206 lbs.
Bats: left
Throws: left
Position: leftfield
Career: 1986–

"**B**onds has a rare combination of power and speed. He is one of four players to have more than 300 home runs and 300 steals."

That was written in 1980 when Barry was 16 years old. How could that be? Easy. The writer was talking about his father, Bobby, who played in the majors from 1968 to 1981. But it could have been about his son also. Only now, Barry has jumped past his father to become the only player ever to hit 400 homers, steal 400 bases in his career, and after the 2000 season, in which he smashed 49 homers and drove in 106 runs, it's clear he is still going strong.

Just like Ken Griffey, Jr., Barry Bonds inherited greatness from one of the best in the game. But while he was born with a great deal of ability, young Barry still had to work hard to develop his talent. And Bobby started his son off early. "Barry was hitting at the age of one year," his father said. "But he perfected his baseball swing at the age of two. By then, he could knock the starch out of the ball." As if that wasn't enough, Barry's godfather would also offer a few pointers. His godfather is the Hall of Famer Willie Mays.

With all that work and advice, Barry hit .467 in his senior year of high school and was drafted by the Giants. But Barry wanted to go to college to polish his game. In three years at Arizona State, he hit .347 and stole 57 bases. At the end of his junior year, he was drafted again. This time he decided to sign. In 1985, he joined the Pittsburgh Pirates' organization.

After years of hearing how good his godfather and his father were, he had something to prove: that he had greatness, too. Over four seasons from 1990 to 1993, he was named the Most Valuable Player three times. The one season he didn't win the award, in 1991, he came in second. No one else has ever had that kind of run.

Bonds did it with an amazing combination of power and speed. In 1990, his first MVP year, he became only the second player to hit more than 30 homers and steal more than 50 bases in a season. He was even better in 1992 and 1993. Both years, he led the majors in slugging with averages of .624 and .677. Among the league leaders he outslugged were the best around: Ken Griffey, Jr., Mark McGwire, Juan Gonzalez, and Frank Thomas.

In '93, he led the National League in homers and home run percentage. He also took the RBI title with 123. Bonds batted .336 that year, good enough for fourth place.

"Willie Mays, Hank Aaron, Mickey Mantle. Their legends grew when their careers ended," said outfielder Brett Butler, who watched many a Bonds home run fly over the fence behind him. "When the numbers come out and Barry is out of the game, then he'll be in that same legend stage. There is no doubt Barry Bonds is the best player in baseball." Phillies catcher Darren Daulton agreed. "It's not even close," he said.

Unlike his father, who struck out so often he has the major league record for most in a single season, Barry has an excellent batting eye for a slugger. His dad had more than 100 strikeouts in a season 10 times. Barry has only done that once.

Bonds might yet hit 500 homers and swipe 500 bases. If he doesn't, maybe his son will.

More Numbers

• Bonds has had over 100 RBIs nine times. It probably would have been ten in a row except the 1994 season was shortened because of a strike. When the season ended after only 112 games, he already had 89 RBIs.
• He has led the league in walks five times. That helped boost his on-base percentage to over .400 for nine years in a row.
• He has led the league in on-base percentage four times.
• He has scored 95 or more runs 12 times.
• Bonds's .557 slugging average is seventh highest among active players, and is eighth all time.

The Rundown

HITS: Three MVPs in four years says it all. His combination of power and speed is the best the game has ever seen.

OUTS: His lifetime .288 average is much lower than that of other greats. He has led the league in RBIs, runs scored, and home runs only once apiece and has never led in hitting.

Dan Brouthers, on an early baseball card.

DAN BROUTHERS

Nickname: Big Dan
Given name: Dennis Joseph Brouthers
Born: May 8, 1858, Sylvan Lake, New York
Died: August 6, 1932
Size: 6'2" 207 lbs.
Bats: left
Throws: left
Position: first base
Career: 1879–1896, 1904

Like Babe Ruth, the slugging Dan Brouthers came to baseball as a pitcher. But unlike the Babe, Brouthers was terrible at it. After just two starts, the team realized the six-foot-two-inch, 207-pound Brouthers belonged in the outfield. It was the right decision. Brouthers with his thick mustache quickly became one of the greats of the nineteenth century.

Because of a tragic accident, Brouthers almost gave up the game before he arrived in the majors. He was playing a game for his local team when he tried to score on a hit. He collided with the catcher, who fell unconscious and soon died. Brouthers was so devastated, he said he would never play again.

Brouthers eventually changed his mind, and he soon became the biggest superstar in nineteenth-century baseball. In the majors, he was a five-time batting champ who also led the league in slugging average six years in a row, from 1881 to 1886.

In 1886, he clouted a ball clear out of Capitol Park in Washington. For many years, it was considered the longest ball ever hit. Once in Baltimore, he hit a ball so hard, a writer wrote it "touched Mother Earth 60 feet from the fence to the outside of the grounds. Then it galloped up Calvert Street and assaulted a Blue Line car." A policeman then found the ball and brought it back to the club. It was hit so far, the Orioles had it bronzed and kept as a souvenir.

Brouthers was the biggest of four star players on the Buffalo Bisons who shook the baseball world to its roots in 1885 when the team traded them to the Detroit Wolverines for much needed cash. The other owners were so angry, they refused to let Brouthers and the others play. But two years later, they changed their minds, and Brouthers led the Wolverines to the championship.

Like Barry Bonds, Brouthers was one of the rare sluggers who also had real speed. He stole 235 bases in his career and had an excellent batting eye. He only struck out 238 times in 6,711 at bats. In contrast, Babe Ruth struck out 1,330 times in 8,399 at bats, that is, 1,092 more strikeouts in just 1,688 more at bats. (For more on sluggers' strikeout-to-hit ratios, see Joe DiMaggio.)

Brouthers was a genuine star in his time, but unlike today's players, stars didn't earn much money back then. When his career was over, Brouthers needed a job. His old friend John McGraw of the New York Giants gave him one as a night watchman and press box custodian for the team. He did that until he died.

More Numbers

• Brouthers batted .300 or over 16 years in a row.
• He won consecutive batting crowns twice: in 1882 and 1883 and again in 1891 and 1892.
• His .349 lifetime batting average is fifth all time.
• He scored over 100 runs eight times, leading the league twice.
• He led the league in hits and doubles three times apiece and in homers twice.
• His 205 triples are eighth all time.
• His lifetime slugging average of .519 is the highest of anyone who played before 1900. He established 68 batting records during his career.

The Rundown

HITS: He was a slugger in an era when players didn't hit a lot of home runs. But he also had surprising speed for a big man. With those qualities, he dominated his era in the same way Babe Ruth and Ty Cobb dominated theirs.

OUTS: He led the league in homers only twice.

Jesse Burkett.

JESSE BURKETT

Nickname: The Crab
Given name: Jesse Cail Burkett
Born: December 4, 1868, Wheeling,
     West Virginia
Died: May 27, 1953
Size: 5'8" 155 lbs.
Bats: left
Throws: left
Position: outfield
Career: 1890–1905

One day, Jesse Burkett stood by the cage to watch the Boston Red Sox take batting practice. They were laying down bunts and not doing a very good job at it. Burkett got disgusted and grabbed a bat. He stepped up to the plate and motioned to the pitcher to toss them in as hard as he could. On the first pitch, Burkett laid a perfect bunt down the third base line. He put the next one down the first base line. With the next pitch, he smoked a line drive over second base.

Nothing unusual, except Burkett was 70 at the time. The next time someone says turn-of-the-century players weren't as good as the modern-day hitters, tell them that story.

At five feet eight inches and 155 pounds, Burkett was small compared to today's players, but like Wee Willie Keeler, he was small compared to turn-of-the-century players, too. He was known as "The Crab," because he had to fight to earn the respect of the bigger guys. He did so by topping .400 twice.

Burkett almost always batted leadoff. That meant he followed the weakest hitters in the lineup. Still, he was a fine RBI man for a little guy, amassing 952 in his career.

Burkett specialized in fouling off pitches as he waited for the one he wanted to hit. He was too good at it. In part because of him, the owners decided to change the rules, so that in 1901 a foul ball became a strike. That didn't matter to Burkett. He still led the league in hitting that year.

More Numbers

• He led the league in hitting three times in his career, in 1895 (.409), 1896 (.410), and 1901 (.382).
• He had more than 200 hits six out of seven consecutive seasons from 1895 to 1901. He missed seven out of seven when he "only" had 198 hits in 1897. Ty Cobb's best consecutive 200-hit string was three times.
• Burkett scored over 100 runs a season nine times.

The Rundown

HITS: He was the perfect singles hitter. He topped .400 twice, and his .342 lifetime average is tied for 11th all time with Babe Ruth and Harry Heilmann. In 1895, he and pitcher Cy Young led the Cleveland Spiders to the Temple Cup. Burkett starred in the championship series by hitting .476.

OUTS: With the exception of 1901, when he hit 10 homers, he had little power. His .400 seasons came when pitchers were still adjusting to the pitching mound being moved back to 60 feet 6 inches.

Roberto Clemente.

ROBERTO CLEMENTE

Given name: Roberto Walker Clemente
Born: August 18, 1934, Carolina,
        Puerto Rico
Died: December 31, 1972
Size: 5'11" 175 lbs.
Bats: right
Throws: right
Position: rightfield
Career: 1955–1972

I t was a typical Roberto Clemente hit—a line drive that whizzed into the gap. Clemente scrambled into second and acknowledged the standing ovation from the Pittsburgh crowd.

That hit off Jon Matlack of the Mets on September 30, 1972, was the 3,000th of his career. It was also his last. Three months later he was dead. Clemente died in an airplane crash. The plane was bringing much needed supplies to Nicaragua, which had just endured an earthquake that had killed hundreds of people. The baseball world felt so much grief when he died, he was named to the Hall of Fame in a special vote.

"I want to be remembered as a ballplayer who gave all he had to give," Clemente had said. He will be. Anyone who saw his play in the 1971 World Series will recall one of the greatest displays of talent ever seen. The Pirates went into the series as underdogs against the Orioles. They lost the first two games, but Clemente in the clubhouse and on the field just refused to let the team lose. He started the scoring off in Game 3, which the Pirates won 5–1. He had three hits in Game 4, and homered in Games 6 and 7 to lead the Pirates to victory.

Clemente hit safely in every game for a .414 average. Games he didn't win with his bat, he helped win with his cannon of an arm in rightfield. For years he played in Pittsburgh where not many people knew about him. But after the '71 Series, everyone was talking about the great Clemente.

"He had about him a touch of royalty," said baseball's commissioner Bowie Kuhn. Clemente's father was the foreman on a sugar plantation in Puerto Rico. Young Roberto was a star in high school. He was so good that 10 major league scouts showed up just for his graduation ceremonies.

He signed with the Dodgers and played with their minor league team for one year. He only hit .257, so the Dodgers decided to leave him unprotected in the draft. They were hoping no one would notice him, but Pittsburgh's clever general manager Branch Rickey (the man who signed Jackie Robinson for the Dodgers) did and stole him for $4,000. He starred for the Pirates for the next 18 years.

Clemente captured four National League batting crowns. Three of those four years, he led both leagues in hitting. His lifetime batting average of .317 was not high compared to that of many other greats, but it was 62 points over the league average during that time. To give you a sense of how good that was, Babe Ruth's lifetime batting average was 67 points higher than the league's. Willie Mays's lifetime average of .302 was 46 points higher than the league's average.

Clemente played most of his career in Forbes Field, which was 457 feet to center and 365 feet to right. This was not a home run hitter's park, but Clemente, like all great hitters, adjusted, in this case by becoming a line drive hitter. Still, Clemente managed to smash 240 round-trippers in his career. If he hadn't cared so deeply for the people of Central America, he would have had many more.

More Numbers

- He hit over .300 13 times, over .340 five times.
- He had over 200 hits in a season four times.
- Clemente was an All-Star 12 times and won the MVP in 1966.

The Rundown

HITS: Clemente was one of the great line drive hitters of the modern era. His .328 average in the 1960s was the highest of any player in the decade.

OUTS: He had only two seasons with more than 100 RBIs and only scored 100 or more runs three times.

Ty Cobb.

TY COBB

Nickname: The Georgia Peach
Given name: Tyrus Raymond Cobb
Born: December 18, 1886, Narrows, Georgia
Died: July 17, 1961
Size: 6'1" 175 lbs.
Bats: left
Throws: right
Position: leftfield
Career: 1905–1928

Ty Cobb was such a great hitter, people told stories about him long after he retired. Lefty O'Doul played during Ty Cobb's day. He liked to tell this story about a dinner he attended in 1960. After he made a speech, a boy asked him what Cobb would hit if he was still playing. "Oh, maybe .340," O'Doul told him.

"Then why do you say Cobb was so great if he could only hit .340?"

"Well," O'Doul answered, "you have to take into consideration the man is 73 years old."

For so many people there is simply no argument—Cobb was the best. And the one who would say it the loudest would be Cobb.

There has never been a competitor like Cobb. He was plain mean on and off the field. He loved it when other players saw him sharpening his spikes before a game, because he knew it would frighten infielders away from one of his hard slides.

Hardly anybody liked Cobb, not even his teammates, but he didn't care. All he cared about was winning. He never gave up. Even when a game was lost, he would try something new because maybe it would teach him something he could use for the next day. That's the kind of thinking that made him the first player elected to the Hall of Fame.

Cobb retired in 1928 after "only" hitting .323 at the age of 41 because he could no longer field well. Imagine how long he would have played had there been a DH! His .367 lifetime batting is the highest all time, nine points ahead of Rogers Hornsby's.

He topped .400 three times. Three other players did that: Jesse Burkett, Hornsby, and Ed Delahanty. But Burkett and Delahanty both hit .400 before a foul ball was considered a strike. That's a huge advantage.

Hornsby's .400 averages were helped by the fact that the game had changed in the 1920s. By then, umpires allowed new balls to be introduced in the middle of a game. They were livelier and cleaner and could be hit much farther. Two of Cobb's .400-plus seasons came in the Dead Ball era when the hitters were at a disadvantage.

But let's not compare him against players of a different era, let's see how he checks out against those he played with. Twelve times, he led the American League in hitting, including nine years in a row, from 1907 to 1915. Nobody has come close to that kind of domination. He won those titles playing against some of the greatest hitters of all time, including Babe Ruth, Shoeless Joe Jackson, Tris Speaker, and Nap Lajoie. Even when he didn't win, he came in second three times, and fourth once. In 1927, he finished fifth with a .357 average, and he was 40 years old.

If Cobb was only a singles hitter, you could dismiss his average and say, "Yeah, he got a lot of hits, but did he produce a lot of runs?" Let's look. Cobb's 2,245 runs are still the major league record, and he played 15 years in an era when low-scoring games were common. Imagine how many he would have scored if he was in his prime in the '20s and '30s when runs were being scored in bunches.

Cobb isn't first on the list of lifetime RBIs. But he is fourth, by far the highest of anyone who played in his era. And again, while he played most of his career in a low-scoring era, he still managed to knock in more than 100 RBIs in a season seven times in his career.

For nearly 50 years, he held the major league record for

career hits with 4,191. Pete Rose passed him in 1985 and finished with 4,256, but Rose got those extra 65 hits with 2,624 more at bats than Cobb had.

Clearly, the one area where he lags behind is in home runs. Cobb only hit 118 during his career, but that was mostly because he played a different style of baseball from that of the big swingers who came along in the 1920s. But don't think he didn't have power. He led the league in slugging average eight times, including six seasons in a row, from 1907 to 1912.

Ruth gripped his bat at the knob and swung from the heels. Cobb choked up on the bat and held his hands a few inches apart. That gave him the bat control he wanted. One day in 1925 he laughed when he was told he didn't have Ruth's power. That day he slid his hands down to the knob of his bat and hit three home runs against the Browns. The next day he hit two more. He proved his point.

Winning was the most important thing to Cobb, and he simply did what he had to do to win. And in his day that wasn't hitting home runs, it was outthinking the opposition. Ted Williams said Cobb was the most intelligent player he ever met. (And not only on the baseball field. Later, Cobb would make millions investing in Coca-Cola when the company was still young.)

Rube Bressler, who played against Cobb, agreed. "Cobb could hit the long ball when he wanted to," Bressler said, "but he didn't. He manipulated. Drove infielders crazy. . . . And he had that terrible fire. I never saw anybody like him. It was his base, his game. Everything was his. The most feared man in the history of baseball."

More Numbers

- He holds the major league record for most years batting over .300—23. Next is Stan Musial with 17.
- He had nine 200-hit seasons (one behind Pete Rose).

- He holds the major league record for most seasons leading the league in hits with eight (one more than Rose).
- Cobb scored more than 100 runs in a season 11 times in his career (two behind Lou Gehrig).
- He led the league in scoring five times (one more than Gehrig).
- Cobb's second in career triples.
- He is fourth in career doubles.
- He is fourth in stolen bases.
- He is fourth in total bases.
- Cobb held 90 batting records when he retired.

The Rundown

HITS: The most competitive player in the history of baseball, and as a hitter there wasn't anything he couldn't do. He had great speed and power. His career batting average will probably never be beaten. Nobody won more batting championships.

OUTS: He didn't hit a lot of home runs.

Ed Delahanty, from an early baseball card.

ED DELAHANTY

Nickname: Big Ed

Given name: Edward James Delahanty

Born: October 30, 1867, Cleveland, Ohio

Died: July 2, 1903

Size: 6'1" 170 lbs.

Bats: right

Throws: right

Position: outfield, second base, first base

Career: 1888–1903

In 1945, baseball writers realized there was a real injustice regarding the Hall of Fame. None of the stars of the nineteenth century were enshrined. Something had to be done immediately, so they began their selection of great players from that period. The first one they chose was Ed Delahanty.

Delahanty almost didn't need to join a major league baseball team. He could have formed one from his own family. They were good players, too. Five of the seven Delahanty brothers eventually made it to the majors. But the greatest of them all was the one they called Big Ed.

Despite playing in the Dead Ball era, Del could electrify the "cranks" (fans) with his slugging. On July 13, 1896, he pulled off one of the great feats of the century when he hit four round-trippers in a game against Chicago. One of his shots went to the deepest part of Philadelphia's Baker Bowl. It would be another 36 years before another player did that again.

When he was with the Phillies from 1891 to 1901, Delahanty was part of the best outfield the game has ever seen. The three fielders were Billy Hamilton, Delahanty, and Sam Thompson. All three would end up in the Hall of Fame.

Delahanty was a bad-ball hitter with a reputation for swinging at anything, whether it was over the plate or not.

"The most dangerous thing to throw that bat-mad galoot is a wild pitch," said one opposing manager. "If you let him get a step into the ball, he'll knock the cover off."

Delahanty wanted to be more patient at the plate, but he couldn't help himself. "If I could only hold myself like that old crab Cap Anson, I would bat better than he ever did, but I can't," Delahanty said. "When the ball seems to me to be coming to my liking, I am going to belt it. I don't care where it comes, I'll either hit it or miss it."

He didn't miss too many. Three times he bettered .400 and came close in 1896 when he batted .397. He led the league in hitting twice, and when he jumped from the National League to the American league in 1902 and captured the American League batting crown, he became the only man in history to win batting titles in both leagues. His .346 lifetime average is sixth all time.

Delahanty was such a fierce hitter that line drives were jokingly called "Delahanty bunts." He once hit a ball so hard it broke into two pieces. Newspaper accounts of the day said it wasn't unusual for a fielder to be sent to the hospital after being broadsided by a Delahanty liner.

He was also fast and was one of the very few players ever to have led the league in both home runs and stolen bases.

Overall, he smashed 100 home runs, which seems low by today's standards, but it was not far off Sam Thompson's then record-setting total of 128.

Sadly, Delahanty's life and career came to an early end. On July 2, 1903, while he was playing for the Senators, the team was traveling by train from Detroit to New York. Delahanty had had too much to drink, and a conductor ordered him off the train. He walked along the tracks and fell through an open drawbridge into the river below and died. His body wasn't found until a week later.

More Numbers

• Delahanty led the league in RBIs three times, and had over 100 in a season seven times.
• His RBIs-per-game average of .80 is ninth all time.
• From 1893 to 1902, he drove in over 100 runs seven times.
• From 1893 to 1895, he averaged 147 runs scored.
• Delahanty led the league in slugging five times.
• He had more than 190 hits in a season seven times.
• He rapped out 40 or more doubles in a season five times and also captured five doubles titles.

The Rundown

HITS: He was one the game's first superstars with both great power and speed. He was one of only four players to hit over .400 three times. He was a consistent run scorer and clutch hitter.

OUTS: He benefited greatly when the pitcher's mound was moved back to 60 feet 6 inches. His .400 years came when pitchers were still adjusting to the distance.

Joe DiMaggio slides into third base.

JOE DIMAGGIO

Nicknames: Joltin' Joe, The Yankee Clipper
Given name: Joseph Paul DiMaggio
Born: November 25, 1914, Martinez, California
Died: March 8, 1999
Size: 6'2" 193 lbs.
Bats: right
Throws: right
Position: centerfield
Career: 1936–1942, 1946–1951

If Joe DiMaggio didn't get seasick, he might not have been a baseball player, and if he didn't hurt his knee, he might not have been a New York Yankee. DiMaggio's father was a San Francisco fisherman. He wanted his son to follow in his shoes. But Joe just couldn't stand being out in a boat all day. Instead, he sold newspapers and played baseball.

Joe starred for a local team called the Seals. In 1933, he had a 61-game hitting streak for them. He was so good several major league teams wanted to sign him. Then one day in 1934, Joe hurt his knee while getting out of a taxicab, and most of the teams dropped out of the bidding. They were afraid he couldn't play anymore.

But a Yankee scout wouldn't give up. "Don't back off because of the kid's knee," the scout told Yankee general manager Ed Barrow. "He'll be all right, and you can get him cheap." The Yankees did, and at $25,000 he was one of the greatest bargains in the history of the game.

Ted Williams of the Red Sox battled against DiMaggio's Yankees for over 10 years. Williams says the Yankee Clipper was the greatest all-around player he ever saw. "At the plate he was poetry in motion; his fluid swing was a thing of beauty. He hit the ball hard. Screeching line drives!"

Williams made a science of hitting. DiMaggio didn't. "There's no skill involved," he said. "Just go up there and swing at the ball."

Maybe DiMaggio was just being modest. That's the way he was. He was not a showy player. He did everything right, but quietly and with dignity, whether it was hitting or fielding. That didn't mean he didn't care about it.

"Baseball was my life," DiMaggio said after he retired. "I was six years old when I started playing baseball. It was all I knew. It was all I ever wanted to know." Like Williams, DiMaggio was a patient hitter. "As a hitter, I am always waiting for the hurler who has trouble getting the ball over the plate," he said.

In his rookie season of 1936, DiMaggio set rookie records for runs and triples. The home run records still belonged to Babe Ruth, but if the Bambino had been a right-handed hitter, he might not have been called the Sultan of Swat. The Babe was facing a rightfield porch at Yankee Stadium that ranged from 296 to 407 feet. DiMaggio generally hit liners to left and left center, where he was staring at distant fences 301 to 466 feet from home plate. It tells you what kind of power DiMaggio had that he still led the league twice in home runs.

The fences were one reason that he is still considered one of the game's great power hitters even though he totaled only 361 lifetime homers. There were other reasons, too. At the peak of his career, he lost three years because he served in World War II. Foot injuries also cost him later in his career and forced him to retire maybe a year or two early.

Still, you look at 361 lifetime home runs and your first reaction is to say "Big deal. That's less than half the number Hank Aaron hit and just more than half of Babe Ruth's total." But DiMaggio had fewer than half the at bats Aaron did and fewer than Ruth, too.

Since his career was relatively short, the best way to evaluate his hitting is to look at his percentages. Take slugging. At .579, he is seventh all time (even if you include active players). That's higher than Aaron and higher than Willie Mays, Mickey Mantle, Rogers Hornsby, and Stan Musial.

The numbers are typical of DiMaggio in terms of records. He holds very few. But he is consistently close to the top in so many areas. For example, there were few better run producers. DiMaggio was fourth all time when it comes to RBIs per game. Behind him in fifth place is Babe Ruth.

For a power hitter, he had a great eye. He struck out only 369 times in his career. That means he struck out an average of once every 18.5 at bats. Babe Ruth struck out once every 6.31 at bats; Hank Aaron, one out of 8.94; Mickey Mantle, one out of 4.73—between every fourth and fifth time he had an at bat; Willie Mays, one out of 7.13; and Ted Williams, who was known for his sharp batting eye, one out of every 10.86 official times at the plate.

Here's another way to look at it. No other power hitter had a ratio of home runs to strikeouts that was so close. DiMaggio had eight more strikeouts than home runs. Ted Williams, who also had a great eye, had 188 more strikeouts than homers, Babe Ruth 616. That's a lot of outs that DiMaggio didn't make.

His lifetime batting average was .325, but DiMaggio left the Yankees to go overseas after 1942 with an average of .341. He led the league in hitting two years in a row, in 1939 when he hit .381 and 1940 when he hit .352.

DiMaggio was often compared to the other great hitter in the American League at the time—Ted Williams. Williams had a higher lifetime batting average than DiMaggio, but Williams also spent his career in little Fenway Park. When they were both playing away from their home parks, DiMaggio outhit Williams, .333 to .328.

In 1948, already suffering from the heel problem that would end his career, DiMaggio still led the league in home runs (39) and RBIs (155).

DiMaggio's heel was so bad it seemed as if his career would be over in 1949. He missed the first 65 games of the season. Meanwhile, it looked like the Red Sox would win the pennant, but DiMaggio came back and hit .346 over the rest of the season with 67 RBIs in only 76 games. In the last week of the season, the Yankees swept the Red Sox three games with Joe hitting four homers and driving in nine runs. It was some of the most spectacular hitting ever seen. Imagine what he would have done had he been healthy.

But you can't talk about DiMaggio's great hitting without talking about the streak—his 56-game hitting streak in 1941. That record that will be around for a while. He didn't just go 1-for-4 during the streak either. He hit .407 over those 56 games.

After he broke Willie Keeler's 44-game mark, he was under huge pressure. But he still hit .575 over the streak's final 10 games. And when it was finally over on July 4, he immediately went on a 16-game hitting streak. The streak occurred the same year that Ted Williams hit .406, but it was DiMaggio who was voted the league's MVP.

More Numbers

• DiMaggio scored over 100 runs a season eight times and knocked in over 100 RBIs his first seven years in the league, leading the league twice. The streak was interrupted by World War II.

• He was an All-Star every year he played and was named MVP three times in his 13-year career. He finished in the top five in voting four other times.

The Rundown

HITS: No power hitter in the history of the game had a better batting eye. His slugging average outpaces his home run totals. He could do it all. He led the league at different times in batting average, slugging, home runs, runs, and RBIs.

OUTS: Others had higher batting averages and/or home run percentages.

Jimmie Foxx.

JIMMIE FOXX

Nicknames: Double X, The Beast
Given name: James Emory Foxx
Born: October 2, 1907, Sudlersville,
　　　　Maryland
Died: July 21, 1967
Size: 6' 195 lbs.
Bats: right
Throws: right
Position: first base
Career: 1925–1942, 1944–1945

Many people think Jimmie Foxx was the strongest man ever to play the game. Old-timers recall one homer the ex-farmboy smashed off Hall of Famer Lefty Gomez that landed in the last row of Yankee Stadium's upper deck. The ball was hit so hard it broke off the back of a seat. Another time, he launched one clear out of Chicago's Comisky Park. The ball touched down some 600 feet from home plate. Now you know why he was called "The Beast." Gomez once said about him, "He wasn't scouted, he was trapped."

Too bad this book isn't about the funniest ballplayers who ever lived. If it was, Gomez would have won easily. When asked about Foxx's home run off him, Gomez told reporters, "I don't know how far it went, but I do know it takes 45 minutes to walk up there."

Mark McGwire holds the record for most home runs in a season with 70, followed by Sammy Sosa (66), McGwire (65), Sosa (63), Roger Maris (61), and Babe Ruth (60). McGwire again (in 1997), Foxx, and Hank Greenberg are next with 58. Foxx hit his in 1932. But consider this. His home field was Shibe Park in Philadelphia. Five times he sent a ball into a screen against the rightfield pavilion that kept the ball in play. That same year, he hit three into the screen in front of leftfield in the Cleveland Indians' League

Park. Both screens had just been put up that season. Those shots would have been home runs other years.

Four times he led the league in home runs. That doesn't seem so much unless you realize his competition included Ruth, Lou Gehrig, Greenberg, and Joe DiMaggio when they were at their peaks.

When Foxx retired in 1945 with 534 home runs, only Babe Ruth had more with 714. His home run percentage is eighth on the all-time list, even though for years he played in Shibe Park. Shibe was not a hitter's park, not with its left- and centerfield fences that ranged from 334 to 447 feet.

Hank Aaron's last productive years were played in Atlanta, which was one of the easiest parks for home run hitters in the majors. Even Yankee Stadium with its short right-field stands was an easier park for a left-handed home run hitter like Ruth.

Like the Babe, Foxx hit for average as well as power. He led the league in hitting twice. In 1933, he won the Triple Crown. He eclipsed .330 nine times. He topped 400 total bases in a season twice. Only Gehrig bettered that mark. Foxx and Gehrig are the only two players who had over 400 total bases two years in a row.

Hank Aaron holds the major league mark for total bases in a career, but he played much longer than Foxx, and later in his career Aaron was also a DH. When you average the number of total bases per game, Foxx's is 2.13. Aaron's is 2.07. Of the top ten in total bases in a career, only Ruth averaged more total bases per game than Foxx. Ruth's is 2.31.

Foxx was the MVP three times, again while competing against the likes of Ruth, Gehrig, Greenberg, Charlie Gehringer, Mickey Cochrane, Al Simmons, and Lefty Grove. All of them became Hall of Famers.

Like the Babe and Gehrig, Foxx knocked in over 100 runs a season 13 times in his career. They are tied for the major league record. Foxx and Gehrig did it 13 years in a row. That's also a record.

Foxx also still holds the American League record for slugging average by a right-handed hitter in a single season, .749. He led the league in slugging five times. His career slugging average of .609 is fourth on the all-time list with only Ruth, Gehrig, and Williams ahead of him.

The Beast was capable of some beastly behavior. How's this for a doubleheader? On July 2, 1933, he hit two homers in the first game, and then hit two in the nightcap. Between them was a double and triple. Reporters who were there say both of those hits were off the top of the outfield wall. He missed hitting six homers in a day by less than a foot.

More Numbers

• Foxx still holds the single-season record for total bases in a season by a right-handed hitter with 438 in 1932.
• His career total of 1,921 RBIs is sixth on the all-time list.
• Foxx holds the major league record for most consecutive years hitting 30 or more home runs with 12.

The Rundown

HITS: He was a tremendously powerful slugger who led the league in slugging five times, hit for average, and with his 13 100-plus RBI seasons was also a great clutch hitter. He won the MVP three times against terrific competition.

OUTS: Others had a higher batting average.

Lou Gehrig.

⚾ LOU GEHRIG

Nicknames: Columbia Lou, The Iron Horse
Given name: Ludwig Heinrich Gehrig
Born: June 19, 1903, New York City
Died: June 2, 1941
Size: 6′ 200 lbs.
Bats: left
Throws: left
Position: first base
Career: 1923–1939

Every baseball fan knows that the 1927 Yankees were one of the greatest—if not the greatest—baseball teams ever assembled. That year they won the pennant over the Philadelphia Athletics—a team with eight future Hall of Famers—by 19 games! It was also the year that Babe Ruth hit 60 home runs in a season. That broke his own mark and established a record that would never be broken in a 154-game season. So who was the MVP that year? Lou Gehrig.

For most of his career, Gehrig played in Ruth's shadow. But, said Gehrig, "it's a pretty big shadow. It gives me lots of room to spread myself." That he did, like pancake batter.

This is the kind of monster year Gehrig had for the greatest team that ever played. He hit .373, third best in the league. He banged 47 homers, second in the league, and knocked in a league-leading 175 runs, ahead of Ruth by nine. He also led the majors in total bases with 447. That figure has been surpassed only twice, by Ruth in 1921 and by Rogers Hornsby in 1922.

"With the exception of Ruth, I don't think any player could have matched Lou Gehrig if Gehrig could have played out his career in good health," said Ted Williams. "Only God knows what he'd have done."

Gehrig first stepped into Ruth's shadow one day in 1923. He came from Columbia University where he was famous for hitting the longest ball anyone had ever seen on the campus. But none of the Yankees had ever heard of him the day he took batting practice with the team for the first time.

By chance, he picked out Babe Ruth's bat from a pile sitting in front of the dugout. Then he walked over to home plate to take his first swings. Nervously, he missed the first two pitches. He bounced the next one weakly to second base. But no one could believe their eyes after Gehrig slammed the next pitch high into the rightfield bleachers. Only the Babe had hit one that far. Three more went to the same spot. The Yankees' manager, Miller Huggins, turned to the players. "The name's Gehrig" was all he said. The players didn't say anything.

Gehrig played briefly for the Yankees in 1923 and 1924. Then, on June 1, 1925, the Yankees regular first baseman, Wally Pipp, complained of a headache. Huggins started Gehrig in his place, and Lou didn't sit out another game until 1939.

They called Gehrig the "Iron Man" for good reason. Through the years, he suffered broken bones, a bad back, a broken toe, and other injuries, but still he never missed a game. His record of 2,130 consecutive games was thought to be unbreakable, and it was until Cal Ripken, Jr., broke it in 1995.

Gehrig was a fearsome hitter. Line drives just whizzed off his bat, especially when there was someone on base. He was a machine when it came to RBIs. He is third all time in RBIs behind Aaron and Ruth. But remember, Aaron played in 1,134 more games than Gehrig. When it comes to RBIs per game, Gehrig is tied for first with Sam Thompson and Hank Greenberg. Aaron is 25th on the list, Ruth fifth. Over 13 seasons, he averaged 149 RBIs a year. Jimmie Foxx, Gehrig's great competition at first base and a great RBI man himself, averaged 132, and Foxx had Al Simmons and Mickey Cochrane, two Hall of Famers, ahead of him in the lineup. Gehrig's 184 in 1931 remains the American League record. The most Ruth ever had in a season was 171.

Gehrig's .632 slugging average is third all time. He is 12th on the list of career total bases with 5,059, but he played in far fewer games than the leaders. Let's look at his total bases per game. Aaron's is 2.08, Gehrig's 2.33. In that sense, he was a more productive hitter than Aaron.

Aaron, of course, hit many more home runs than Gehrig did, 755 to 493, but his .555 slugging percentage is far behind Gehrig's. Gehrig also beats him in home run percentage. That's the number of home runs per 100 at bats. Gehrig's is 6.2, Aaron's 6.1.

And then there is hitting in the clutch, surely a sign of a great hitter. Gehrig has the record for grand slam home runs in his career with 23. Gehrig was also amazing in World Series play, when the games were really on the line. Most baseball fans know the story of Babe Ruth calling his shot in the 1932 World Series against the Cubs. The Yanks swept the Cubs in that classic, but Ruth wasn't the MVP. It was Gehrig. He was simply on fire. In 17 at bats, he had two walks, nine hits, three home runs, and eight RBIs for an average of .529. His slugging average was 1.118. No one has ever come even close to that.

How does he compare with Ruth over the course of his career? As a home run hitter, he doesn't. Ruth has more and his home run percentage is higher, 8.5 to 6.2, but Ruth's lifetime batting average is only two points higher than Gehrig's. If you take away the year that Gehrig was obviously suffering from the disease that would kill him, his average leapfrogs over the Babe's to .344. Gehrig's RBIs per game were higher than Ruth's, and his runs-per-game percentage was also slightly higher.

How was he rated against those he played with? Remember, Gehrig played against many of the best players who ever lived. That includes the likes of Foxx, Hank Greenberg, Bill Terry, and George Sisler, the greatest first basemen of all time. Yet for seven of the full 13 years he was in the league, Gehrig was named the major league's outstanding first baseman by the *Sporting News.* Two times during his career he was named the Most Valuable Player.

The awful truth though about Gehrig was that in the end he wasn't an iron man. In 1938, his production slipped badly, but no one knew anything was wrong until the spring of 1939 when he could barely hit the ball out of the infield, and he was so slow fielding around first base that he once got a big hand just for catching an easy line drive.

It got so bad that on May 2, 1939, he took himself out of the lineup. The streak was over. He never played again. A few days later, he went to the doctor for a checkup. He was told he had an incurable disease, an illness that is still known as Lou Gehrig's disease.

But he was still a hero. Although he knew he was dying, on July 4, 1939, he stood before a sellout crowd in Yankee Stadium and declared he was "the luckiest man on the face of the earth." That may not have made him the best hitter who ever lived, but it says something about his character that is much, much more important.

More Numbers

• He holds the major league record with Ruth and Foxx for most years with 100 or more RBIs with 13.

• Gehrig shares the record with Jimmie Foxx for most consecutive years with 100 or more RBIs.

• He and Babe Ruth hold the major league record for most consecutive years with 150 or more RBIs with three.

• Five times he totaled over 400 bases in a season. The next highest is Willie McCovey with three.

• For 13 straight years he had over 300 total bases in a season, another record.

• Gehrig holds the American League record for most years scoring 100 or more runs.

• He and Hank Aaron are tied for the major league record for the most consecutive years scoring 100 or more runs with 13.

The Rundown

HITS: You want someone who is going to score runs and drive them home. No one did both better than Lou Gehrig, not even Babe Ruth. He hit .344 when healthy, higher than Ruth, and had a better home run percentage and slugging average than Hank Aaron. He outslugged Ty Cobb and won two MVP awards against maybe the best group of players in the game's history.

OUTS: He didn't hit as many home runs as Aaron or Ruth. His batting average was lower than Cobb's.

Hank Greenberg.

⚾ HANK GREENBERG

Nickname: Hammerin' Hank
Given name: Henry Benjamin Greenberg
Born: January 1, 1911, New York City
Died: September 4, 1986
Size: 6'3½" 215 lbs.
Bats: right
Throws: right
Position: first base, outfield
Career: 1930, 1933–1941, 1945–1947

When it comes to judging who belongs at the top of the list of hitters, Hank Greenberg may be the biggest puzzle of all. Hammerin' Hank played only nine full seasons in the majors. Dozens of players have better career stats than Hank. His 331 lifetime home runs don't even rank him among the top 50 all time. His 1,276 RBIs aren't among the top 75. Yet, there isn't an old-timer who won't tell you that Hammerin' Hank wasn't one of the greatest ever.

"Hank Greenberg could do it all," said Ted Williams. "He hit the ball a ton, crushed it like few have ever done. The impact he made in just 1,394 games is nothing short of amazing." Williams went on to say that Greenberg was one of the most intelligent people he ever met in baseball, and his intelligence was one of the keys to his success.

Greenberg grew up in New York City. He was already six feet three when he turned 13. He towered over the other kids, and the ball field was one of the few places where he felt comfortable with himself. But he was not a natural athlete. He had to work at it, and he did, in part because he was less self-conscious when he was playing ball.

He became an excellent high school baseball player, but when he approached his favorite team, the Giants, for a tryout, they refused. They said he was too awkward to have much of a future.

In 1929, a Yankee scout did want to sign him, but Greenberg knew the Yankees already had a pretty good first baseman in Lou Gehrig, so when the Detroit Tigers offered him a contract, he signed with them.

Greenberg was the second major leaguer to enter the service for World War II and lost nearly five years at the peak of his career. That means you have to toss out Greenberg's career numbers when you evaluate him. Instead, you have to look at percentages in order to put his greatness into the proper context.

When asked about what made a great hitter, Greenberg always insisted that RBIs were the most important. "That was my goal—get the man in. Runs batted in are more important than batting average, more important than home runs, more important than anything. That's what wins ball games: driving runs across the plate."

Greenberg is in a virtual tie with Gehrig and Sam Thompson for the highest RBIs-per-game percentage in history. His 183 RBIs in 1937 are the third highest ever recorded. And the Tigers did win a lot of games when Greenberg was with them. From 1933 to 1940, they won four pennants and finished second twice. They had one of the best hitting teams of all time. In 1934, their infield of Greenberg, Charlie Gehringer, Billy Rogell, and Marv Owen batted in 462 runs, a major league record.

The 1940 team was nearly as good. That year, Greenberg led the league in slugging, homers, and RBIs, and he credited his fine season to his manager for an unusual reason. The manager, Del Baker, was known as the best sign stealer in baseball. Standing in the third base coach's box, he would relay the catcher's signs to Greenberg, telling him when to expect a fastball and when to expect a curve. "I loved that," Greenberg said. "I was the greatest hitter in the world when I knew what kind of pitch was coming up."

Over his nine seasons, he led the league in RBIs four times. That's 44 percent of his career. Lou Gehrig is considered the game's leading RBI man. He led the league in RBIs five times. That's 36 percent of his full 14 seasons. Babe Ruth led the league six times in 16 full seasons of plate appearances. That's 38 percent.

Greenberg also won four home run titles in his nine seasons. Two of those homers provided the greatest thrills in his career. Greenberg returned to the majors from the Air Force on July 1, 1945. That day, 50,000 came to the ballpark to welcome him back, and he hit a home run to help win the ball game. Then, on the last day of the season, the Tigers needed a win to clinch the pennant. They were playing the Browns, who took a one-run lead into the ninth inning. But the Tigers loaded the bases with one out. Up to the plate came Greenberg. With the count 1-1, he sent the next pitch into the bleachers for a grand slam home run to give Detroit the pennant. He then hit two homers and knocked in seven runs to help lead the team to the world championship over the Cubs.

Greenberg's greatest home run season was back in 1938 when he nearly tied Babe Ruth's record of 60. With five games left in the season, he had 58. But he failed to get another. Greenberg said he simply "ran out of gas."

Greenberg didn't have a lot of speed, and he had to work hard to become the excellent hitter and fielder he was. He was not a natural athlete. But he also had to overcome another handicap. He was a Jewish player at a time when anti-Semitism was common in America. He was thrown at often by opposing pitchers and was the subject of many cruel comments by opposing players.

Greenberg wasn't very religious, but one year the Tigers were in the pennant race, and a crucial game was scheduled the same day as Rosh Hashanah, the Jewish New Year. Greenberg didn't want to play, but he talked it over with some rabbis, and they found an ancient biblical reference to ball-playing. They said that meant it was okay for him to play.

But eight days later, a game fell on Yom Kippur, the holiest of Jewish holidays. This time he refused to play. Though the Tigers lost, the poet Edgar Guest had this to say:

> *We shall miss him in the infield*
> *And we shall miss him at the bat*
> *But he's true to his religion,*
> *And I honor him for that.*

More Numbers

- He won the MVP twice.
- Greenberg scored over 100 runs six times in his nine full seasons.
- His .605 lifetime slugging average is fifth all time.

The Rundown

HITS: If you go by the percentages, he is the greatest RBI man of all time. He also won four home run crowns in his limited career.

OUTS: His lifetime .313 batting average might have been higher if he had more speed. Others had much longer playing careers.

Ken Griffey, Jr.

KEN GRIFFEY, JR.

Given name: George Kenneth Griffey, Jr.
Born: November 21, 1969, Donora,
Pennsylvania
Size: 6'3" 195 lbs.
Throws: left
Bats: left
Position: centerfield
Career: 1989–

L ike Barry Bonds, Ken Griffey, Jr., was born to play baseball. And like Bonds, he has proven to be better than his father. Ken Sr. hit 152 home runs in his career. Ken Jr. turned 30 in 1999 and was the youngest player in the history of the game to reach 350 homers.

It took Bonds about five years to make a major impact on the league. It took Griffey about five minutes. Ken Jr. was all of 19 when he made the Seattle roster in 1989 after he hit .359 that spring. Until he broke his finger in July, he was leading all rookies with 13 homers and 45 RBIs.

The next year his career really took off when he finished in the top ten in total bases, hits, batting, triples, and slugging. And he was only 20 years old.

But maybe the best day of the season for him had nothing to do with his own numbers. On August 31, he took his usual position out in centerfield. Then he looked over to the leftfielder, a newcomer to the team, and gave him a smile. How could he not? The leftfielder was his father.

A father and son had never played together in the majors before. "It seemed like a father-son game to me," Ken Jr. said after the game, "like we were out in the backyard playing catch."

They had been doing that for nearly 20 years. Young Ken was a regular in the Cincinnati Reds dugout when his dad was a star with the Big Red Machine in the 1970s. Ken Sr. was 39 and still playing when his son made the Mariners in 1989. Then he joined the team for a year in 1990.

"You can talk about the 1976 batting race, the two World Series I played in, and the All-Star Games, but this is number one," he said. "This is the best thing that's ever happened to me."

Ken Sr. was a terrific ballplayer. He was a steady line drive hitter who hit .296 over 19 years. But like Barry and Bobby Bonds, the son is clearly better. When his career is over, Ken Jr. just may well be the best ever.

In 1998, Griffey became the third player to drive in 140 or more runs three seasons in a row. The other two were Babe Ruth and Lou Gehrig. That year Griffey hit 56 round-trippers for the second year in a row. If he had had one more dinger in 1996 to add to his 49, he would have hit at least 53 straight times. His 56 homers were the most for an American Leaguer since Roger Maris's 61 four-baggers broke Ruth's mark in 1961. His league-leading 48 homers in 1999 and his 40 in 2000 weren't too shabby either.

His slugging average of .568 places him eighth on the all-time list.

Do you think Ken is impressed? "I just try and stay consistent and do what I love to do," he says.

More Numbers

• He has scored over 100 runs five times and has passed the 100 mark in RBIs eight times.
• In 1997, he was named the league's MVP.
• Griffey has been elected to the All-Star Game 11 times in his first 12 years.

The Rundown

HITS: He is on his way toward breaking Hank Aaron's career home run record. He is also an excellent RBI man, averaging over 135 RBIs the last four seasons.

OUTS: Other greats had higher batting averages. While he has led the league in homers, he has not ever led the league in RBIs, runs scored, or slugging.

Tony Gwynn.

⚾ TONY GWYNN

Given name: Anthony Keith Gwynn
Born: May 9, 1960, Los Angeles, California
Size: 5′11″ 185 pounds
Bats: left
Throws: left
Position: rightfield
Career: 1982–

When you watch Tony Gwynn stroll up to the plate, it's hard to imagine this is one of the game's greatest hitters. He has a belly and is shaped more like a weekend couch potato, but then you see the muscular legs, quick wrists, and razor-sharp eyes in action, and you quickly know you are watching one great athlete.

This will tell you all you need to know: Gwynn was such a good basketball player at San Diego State University in the 1970s, he still holds the record for most assists. He was so good he was drafted by the NBA's San Diego Clippers on the same day he was drafted by the baseball Padres.

Do you think he made the right choice? In 1997, he won his fourth straight batting title and his eighth overall. That ties him with Honus Wagner for the National League record.

His .338 lifetime average is the highest among all active players. He has also topped .300 for 17 straight years. Only Ty Cobb and Stan Musial have longer streaks. But Gwynn is still going.

Gwynn hit over .350 for five straight years from 1993 to 1997. Only Cobb, Rogers Hornsby, and Al Simmons have done that, but league averages were much higher when they were playing. A big reason is that when Cobb played relief pitching wasn't what it is today. As the introduction explains, in Cobb's day, a relief pitcher was a starter who couldn't pitch well anymore, so he was banished to the bullpen. Cobb didn't have to face pitchers like Rob Nen or Mariano Rivera, whose fastballs can approach 100 mph. In Gwynn's era, closers such as Bruce Sutter and Dennis Eckersley win the Cy Young Award as the best pitcher.

There are also specialists for every kind of situation. Pitchers are expert in throwing against left-handers or right-handers or in middle relief. None of this existed in Cobb's time, and it makes today's game that much tougher.

True, Cobb had disadvantages. There were only eight teams in the league, so the competition was tougher. He also had to face spitballers and he played in the Dead Ball era, but there are plenty of pitchers who do things to the balls today. They nick them with their belt buckles or put grease on them from their hair or their gloves—they just do it illegally.

Whenever anyone compares players of different eras it is important to remember how the game has changed. That's what makes Gwynn's numbers so amazing. His .368 average from 1993 to 1997 is the eighth-highest five-year average in history. Nobody playing now is even close.

And Cobb, Hornsby, and Simmons were all in their twenties when they began their streaks. Gwynn was 33. Ted Williams hit .388 at the age of 39, but he never had five years of hitting over .350. Williams hit .406 in 1941. Who has had the next highest single-season average since then? You guessed it. Gwynn with .394 in 1994. He has the sixth, seventh, eighth, and eleventh highest averages, too.

Gwynn has led the league in hits seven times; only Pete Rose has done that. He has made the *Sporting News* All-Star team six times and has been voted to 16 All-Star Games. Pretty good for a guy who looks like he spends most of his days in front of the TV.

But make no mistake about it. Gwynn is not only physically gifted, he is also smart and he is always thinking at the plate, and he probably works harder at the science of hitting than any other player in the league. Each day, he watches videotapes of his own swing and of opposing pitchers. When he steps into the batter's box, he is prepared. In that sense he is a throwback to the old ballplayers. Back then players' salaries were low, and on the road there was little to do, so they often would occupy themselves by sitting around the hotel lobby talking baseball. The hitters would discuss opposing pitchers for hours. They knew what they would throw and when they would throw it. Gwynn does the same thing, only he uses videotape to get the information he needs. "People have to give me credit for my work ethic, even though I don't look like I have much of one," he said.

Padres president Larry Lauchino is someone who appreciates his star no matter what he looks like. "It reminds me of what they said about General Grant's drinking: 'Give me generals who all drink the same thing.' Well, I'll take players with the same diet as Tony's."

But there is more to his success. And it's a lesson that can be applied anywhere, not just in sports. As a young hitter, he also asked questions. "If Cincinnati was here, I'd be sitting on the bench watching Pete Rose take batting practice, then asking him about hitting," he says. "Man, I was a pest."

More Numbers

- He raised his lifetime batting average from 1993 to 1997, after he was 33 years old. No one has hit as well for average at that age.
- Gwynn reached 3,000 hits in 2,284 games. Only two players got there faster: Ty Cobb (2,135 games) and Nap Lajoie (2,224).

The Rundown

HITS: Clearly, he is the best hitter for average of his time. He dominates batting races in the way Cobb and Wagner did in their prime. Other greats had about the same batting average, but he plays in what may be a much tougher era.

OUTS: He's not a great run producer. He has scored over 100 runs in a season only twice. He only has one season where he knocked in over 100 RBIs. He doesn't hit with a lot of power.

HARRY HEILMANN

Harry Heilmann.

Nickname: Slug
Given name: Harry Edwin Heilmann
Born: August 3, 1894, San Francisco,
        California
Died: July 9, 1951
Size: 6'1" 195 lbs.
Bats: right
Throws: right
Position: leftfield
Career: 1914, 1916–1930, 1932

Harry Heilmann became a baseball player because one day he forgot his coat. It happened on a Saturday afternoon in 1913. Heilmann was a 19-year-old bookkeeper for a biscuit company. That day he decided to go out for a walk. But soon after he stepped outside, he realized he didn't have his coat, so he turned and walked back toward the office. On his way, Heilmann bumped into an old friend, who was managing a local ball club. The friend told him his third baseman was out sick. Could Heilmann fill in? He'd get $10 plus expenses.

Heilmann said yes. That afternoon, he hit a double in the 11th inning to give his team the victory. Fans passed the hat for their new hero. When he totaled up the money, he had made $160. That was more than a regular month's wages at the biscuit company. He was convinced. Soon, he signed a contract (his signing bonus was a spaghetti dinner), and three years later he was in the major leagues.

Rogers Hornsby was known for his long smooth swing. Heilmann's was the opposite. He held the bat low and used a short, choppy swing to produce line drives from a slight crouch. It worked for him. Hornsby had his five great years from 1921 to 1925. Harry Heilmann had a similar run, but he did it every other year. Between 1921 and 1927, but skipping a year, how are these numbers?: .394 in 1921, .403 in

1923, .393 in 1925, and .398 in 1927. All in all, over those four years, he was just nine hits shy of averaging .400.

Each of those years, he won the batting championship. He beat out some of the best hitters who ever lived in the process. That's why he ranks among them. And in between those brilliant years he didn't hit too badly either. He averaged .356 in his off years.

Heilmann didn't start off his career so well. He averaged only .266 his first four years. Why did he suddenly catch fire? Two words: Ty Cobb. When Cobb became manager of the Tigers in 1921, he taught Heilmann how to move his hands up and down the bat and how to distribute his weight better in the batter's box. He also taught him how to get hits from an inside-out swing. "From then on, I was never afraid to get two strikes on me," Heilmann said years later. "I could wait that much longer and still inside-out it and get the big part of the bat on the ball enough to drive it over the infielders."

Cobb also taught him the importance of studying pitchers for weaknesses. He must have spotted a lot of them. In 1921, he nosed out his teacher for the batting crown, hitting .394 to Cobb's .389. He also led the league with 237 hits. In 1923, he reached .403. This time he bested Babe Ruth, who was second at .393 and enjoying one of his best years in the majors.

In 1925, Heilmann proved his toughness when he picked up 50 points on league leader Tris Speaker in September. Then on the last day of the season, the Tigers were playing a doubleheader. In the opener, Heilmann lashed three hits to pass Speaker. His teammates urged him to sit out the second game so he would automatically win the crown, but he refused.

"I'm playing out the string," he said. And that game he went 3-for-3 and beat Speaker for the title by four points, .393 to .389.

Then, in 1927, he was matched against another Hall of Fame hitter, Al Simmons. On the last day of the season, he was again in second place and again playing a doubleheader. In the first game he smashed four hits, including a home run. He was now a point ahead of Simmons. Again, his teammates told him to sit and again he refused. This time he added three more hits to finish six points above Simmons. That's clutch hitting, not once, but four times.

By 1929, arthritis had settled into his wrist, and he had trouble hitting. That year he batted only .344. When he was healthy, there were few better. "People nowadays just don't realize how great a hitter Harry was," said Cobb, years after he retired. "Next to Rogers Hornsby, he was the best right-handed hitter of them all."

Let's look at Heilmann's four best years when he led the league. Over those four years, he averaged .397. If he had nine more hits over that span, he would have reached .400 four

	Average	Hits	Home Runs	RBIs	Slugging	Runs
Heilmann (1921, 1923, 1925, 1927)	.397	874	64	507	.606	438
Cobb (1910–1913)	.398	838	27	392	.570	442
Hornsby (1921, 1922, 1924, 1925)	.406	915	127	515	.703	526
Ruth (1920, 1921, 1923, 1924)	.381	781	200	560	.799	629

times. We can use a chart to compare Heilmann's best four years with Hornsby's, Cobb's, and Ruth's best four.

Against three of the best hitters who ever lived, Heilmann didn't do too badly. He was not as productive as Ruth, but he had a higher average and more hits. Cobb suffers the most in this comparison, but in his defense, his best four years were in the Dead Ball era. That's why his homers and RBIs are lower than the others.

Was Heilmann the best? Maybe yes, maybe no. But if it was the last game of the season and the title was on the line, who would you want at bat?

More Numbers

• His lifetime average is .342, tied with Ruth for 11th all time.
• He had over 200 hits four times.
• Heilmann had eight seasons with more than 100 RBIs.

The Rundown

HITS: In his four best years, he matched up with the best, including Ruth, Cobb, Speaker, and Gehrig, and beat them in the batting race.

OUTS: In his other years, while he was a terrific hitter, his numbers just aren't as good.

Rogers Hornsby.

ROGERS HORNSBY

Nickname: Rajah
Born: April 27, 1896, Winters, Texas
Died: January 5, 1963
Size: 5′11″ 175 lbs.
Bats: right
Throws: right
Position: second base
Career: 1915–1937

R ogers Hornsby was very serious when it came to hitting. How serious? He refused to read newspapers (except the racing pages) or go to the movies out of fear they would hurt his batting eye. A lot of players liked to play golf on their off days. Hornsby didn't. "When I hit a ball, I want somebody else to chase it," he said.

They did. Many people who saw him play say he was the greatest right-handed hitter of all time. They may be right. Just look at the five years Hornsby had from 1921 through 1925. In that stretch he batted .397, .401, .384, .424, and .403. That means he averaged .402. No one in major league history has even come close to a streak like that. Even in Cobb's best five years, from 1910 to 1914, he averaged .394. (See the chart in the previous chapter to compare his best four years with the best four seasons of other greats.)

But he didn't just hit for average in those years. He dominated everything. Take 1921, for example. That year, he led the National League in batting, total bases, hits, runs, slugging, RBIs, doubles, triples, and was second in home runs.

In 1922, he topped the league in batting, homers, and RBIs, but he didn't stop at the Triple Crown; he also led in slugging, total bases, hits, runs, and doubles.

Ruth's most dominating year was either 1920 or 1924. In 1920, he led the league in runs, slugging, home runs, RBIs, and walks. In 1924, he was first in batting, total bases, runs, walks, slugging, and home runs. Neither matches Hornsby.

The year before Hornsby's great streak began wasn't too shabby either. He hit .370 to lead the league. He also led the league in slugging, hits, doubles, and RBIs.

Hornsby's theory of hitting was simple: "Get a good ball to hit." He must have had a lot. Seven times in his career he hit .380 or over. Only Cobb topped that.

Hornsby's 250 hits in 1922 are still a National League record for a right-hander. In 1925, he set the National League record for the highest slugging average in a season, .756. It still stands. Even Mark McGwire when he hit his 70 homers in 1998 couldn't beat that. Hornsby's 422 total bases in 1922 also still stands as the National League record. And consider this: Hornsby was a right-handed hitter—a clear disadvantage.

Hornsby's lifetime batting average, .358, is second on the all-time list behind Cobb but 16 points ahead of Ruth's .342. Hornsby didn't only hit for average. He led the league in slugging percentage nine times. That's another National League record. Aaron did it four times; Cobb eight. His career slugging average is .577, eighth on the all-time list. The only player from his era ahead of him is Ruth.

Hornsby's slugging percentage puts him ahead of the greatest home run hitters ever, including Willie Mays, Mickey Mantle, Hank Aaron, and Ralph Kiner. It is behind McGwire's, but Mac's numbers should decline with age.

Although he came up in the Dead Ball era, he quickly became one of the leading power hitters in the 1920s. He hit 42 home runs in 1922 to lead the National League and led the league again in 1925 with 39. He hit 301 homers in his career. No other hitter from that era showed that kind of power. Cobb hit only 118 home runs during his career. Hornsby matched Cobb by leading the league four times in RBIs. He led the National League in runs five times.

No wonder he was so confident as a hitter. "Every time I stepped up to the plate, I couldn't help but feel sorry for the pitcher," he said. He had good reason to.

More Numbers

- Hornsby won six straight batting titles.
- He led the league in triples twice and in walks three times.
- He won the MVP twice.
- When he retired, he held the National League record for lifetime home runs.

The Rundown

HITS: He hit for average. He hit for power. He had speed. He produced runs. He did it all. His five-year run from 1921 to 1925 is one of the greatest ever, if not the greatest. He had more power than Cobb and had a higher average than Ruth.

OUTS: He didn't quite have Ruth's power, and his average was a little lower than Cobb's.

"Shoeless" Joe Jackson.

JOE JACKSON

Nickname: Shoeless Joe
Given name: Joseph Jefferson Jackson
Born: July 16, 1889, Pickens County,
    South Carolina
Died: December 5, 1951
Size: 6'1" 200 lbs.
Bats: right
Throws: right
Position: leftfield
Career: 1908–1920

There are few sadder stories among the greatest hitters of all time than Joe Jackson's. Shoeless Joe, they called him. He was from the backcountry of South Carolina, and he couldn't read or write a lick. The one thing he could do, though, was hit. In 1911, he became the only rookie in the history of the game to hit over .400. He hit .408.

Writers who saw him would say he was the greatest natural hitter ever to play the game. But in 1919, Jackson was part of a plan by eight members of the Chicago White Sox to lose the World Series on purpose to the Cincinnati Red Stockings so that certain gamblers would win their bets. The players did it for the money, and for that they will forever be known as the Chicago Black Sox. It was the worst scandal in the history of the game.

The truth is we don't know how much Jackson took part in the plot. He hit .375 during the Series. Everybody agrees he played well, but he also admitted to taking money from the gamblers.

Jackson was one of the game's great heroes at the time. But during the trial, he broke the country's heart when a little boy approached him on the courthouse steps and said to him, "Say it ain't so, Joe." And he couldn't.

A year later the commissioner of baseball threw him and seven other teammates out of the game forever. In his last year, he hit .382, and he was just approaching his peak.

When you talk about great hitters, the worst you can say about Jackson is that in many categories he was second to Ty Cobb. Actually, when it comes to lifetime batting average, his .356 was third behind Cobb and Rogers Hornsby. But Jackson did outslug Cobb .518 to .513, even though Cobb played well into the lively ball era, which began in 1921. That was the year after Jackson was tossed from the game.

Ted Williams says Jackson, who liked to use a 48-ounce bat he called "Black Betsy," was a better hitter than Cobb. Unlike Cobb and other hitters from the Dead Ball era, Jackson kept his hands together at the knob of the bat and swung hard. Jackson would stand deep in the plate with his feet close together. He wasn't a place hitter like Cobb. Instead, he would slash his classic line drives with a long even swing. "He had the sweetest swing imaginable," said Williams. "For me, Jackson's hitting style was vastly superior to Cobb's."

Jackson had such a perfect swing that a rookie in 1914 did the best he could to copy it. The player was Babe Ruth. "I copied Jackson's batting style because I thought he was the greatest hitter I had ever seen. I still think the same way," the Babe said in 1942.

Jackson hit line drives that actually scared fielders, who would duck away from them. The writer Ring Lardner once took a frightening cab ride to the ballpark. After watching Jackson hit a home run and a double that afternoon, he wondered which would be more dangerous, "to ride in a St. Louis taxicab or play the outfield or infield against Mr. Jackson because you are bound to get killed sooner or later either way."

Tris Speaker is regarded as one of the best centerfielders of all time. But he was once injured when he was hit in the neck by a Jackson line drive because he couldn't get his glove up in time to catch the ball.

"He could break bones with his shots," pitcher Ernie

Shore said. "Blindfold me and I could still tell you when Joe Jackson hit the ball. It had a special crack." The fireballer Walter Johnson, who many say was the best pitcher of all time, faced Jackson on many occasions. He said Jackson had no weaknesses at the plate. Indeed, Jackson's lifetime average against Johnson was .500.

Jackson was still improving on his lifetime average when he was banned from the game. We can only imagine how much his average would have jumped in the next few years.

But we can see how Jackson competed against the players of his own era. In his 10 full years in the league, he was among the top five in batting seven times. That's 70 percent of the time. He hit over .370 four of those 10 years. He led the league in triples three times, so he had speed. You can also see that in the 202 bases he stole.

The biggest question about him was his role in the 1919 Series. Until his death, Jackson said he played as hard as he could in the Series. The numbers support him. He hit .375. His 12 hits set a Series record. He drove in six runs, scored five, and had 16 putouts in leftfield with no errors.

He did take money from gamblers, but he tried to return the money. He also attempted to tell the White Sox owner, Charlie Comisky, what was happening, but Comisky wouldn't talk to him. At that point, he told his manager that he didn't want to play in the Series, but his manager would have none of it, so, playing on pride, Jackson defied the gamblers and went out and played his best.

When he did, there was hardly anything he couldn't do, except say it wasn't so.

More Numbers

• His lifetime slugging percentage of .518 is well behind the all-time leaders. But among the people he played with, it is the highest.

The Rundown

HITS: He was a great line drive hitter when most players didn't hit nearly as hard. Imagine how he would have hit in the lively ball era.

OUTS: He didn't hit many home runs and had fewer RBIs and runs scored than others.

Willie Keeler.

WILLIE KEELER

Nickname: Wee Willie
Given name: William Henry Keeler
Born: March 3, 1872, Brooklyn, New York
Died: January 1, 1923
Size: 5'4½" 140 lbs.
Bats: right
Throws: right
Position: rightfield
Career: 1892–1910

Wee Willie Keeler is still more famous for something he said than for what he did on the baseball field. To Willie, the secret to good hitting was simple: "Hit 'em where they ain't." In other words, find a spot between the fielders and use bat control to place the ball there.

Keeler was one of the smallest players in the majors at only five feet four and a half inches tall. But he followed his own advice so well for 19 years that he averaged .343. Willie learned he didn't have to hit long balls to excel. He probably had the greatest bat control of any player who ever lived. If the infield played deep, he bunted. If they played in, he hit it by them. He and John McGraw played for the Baltimore Orioles in the 1890s, one of the craftiest teams ever to play the game. They won because they were smart—and sometimes a little dirty, to tell the truth. To give you an example, in those days there were usually only two umpires. If the opposing team hit the ball safely into the outfield, the umpire would follow the ball. While the ump's back was turned, one of the Orioles would grab the base runner by the belt and hold on to him so he couldn't run.

While he was with Baltimore, Keeler perfected a way to get a hit by choking up almost halfway up a bat that at 30 inches was already probably the smallest in major league history. Keeler would then bang the ball straight down into the ground, which would cause it to bounce high in the air. By the time it came down, he was already standing on first. The tactic was so successful, it got its own name: the Baltimore chop.

How successful was he? In 1897, his greatest year, he batted .424. He had 239 hits. That was a record until it was broken by Ty Cobb in 1911. His .424 average is the fourth highest ever recorded. His 202 singles in 1898 are still a major league record, and he played in only 128 games!

In 1897, Willie went 2-for-5 on opening day. For the next 43 games, he got at least one hit. His 44-game hitting streak was the major league record until it was broken by Joe DiMaggio in 1941.

His lifetime average of .345 is tied for seventh all time with Tris Speaker. Ed Delahanty and Billy Hamilton were the only players of the 1890s who hit higher, but Willie had more hits than either of them. The only thing he didn't have was their size. "He was just a little tiny guy," said Hall of Famer Sam Crawford about Keeler. "Just a little snap swing, and he'd punch the ball over the infield. You couldn't strike him out. He'd always hit the ball somewhere. And he could fly to first!"

More Numbers

• He smacked over 200 hits eight years in a row.
• Keeler batted over .300 13 years in a row.
• He topped .370 five times.
• Keeler scored over 100 runs eight years in a row.
• Twice, he scored over 160 runs.

The Rundown

HITS: If you just needed a single, he was your man. Keeler was one of the cleverest place hitters in baseball history. He still holds the record for most singles in a season.

OUTS: He had no power, and he had his best seasons soon after the pitching mound was moved back, and the pitchers were still adjusting to the distance.

Nap Lajoie.

NAP LAJOIE

Nickname: Larry
Given name: Napoleon Lajoie
Born: September 5, 1874, Woonsocket,
    Rhode Island
Died: February 7, 1959
Size: 6'1" 195 lbs.
Bats: right
Throws: right
Position: second base
Career: 1896–1916

Today, kids in their Air Jordans and Gap jeans argue about who is the best player, Mark McGwire or Ken Griffey. Well, a hundred years ago, kids in knickers and high-button shoes had their own debates. Except theirs were over Nap Lajoie (pronounced LA-jo-AY) versus Honus Wagner.

Most experts still say that Wagner was one of the greatest players in the history of any sport. That gives you a pretty good idea about the kind of player Lajoie was.

Not everyone thought so at first. When Lajoie signed his first minor league contract, the Phillies sent one of their players to scout him. His report was not positive. "He'll never learn to hit," Tommy McCarthy told his manager. Three years later, no one was arguing whether Tommy McCarthy was better than Honus Wagner.

Lajoie was big and strong. He was a right-handed hitter known for an odd habit of crossing his back leg behind his front one before stepping into a pitch and smashing a line drive over third base. A lot of them must have been doubles. His 658 doubles are sixth on the all-time list.

Cy Young won 511 games over the course of his career. There weren't many hitters he couldn't master, but he didn't like to face Lajoie. "Lajoie was one of the most rugged hitters I ever faced," Young said long after he retired. "He'd take your leg off with a line drive, turn the third baseman around like a swinging door, and powder the hand of the leftfielder."

Lajoie is 12th all time in hits with 3,244. Of the players from his era, only Wagner had more, with 3,418, but Wagner also played in 300 more games than Lajoie did.

In 1901, Lajoie created a huge controversy when he became the first superstar to jump to the newly formed American League. Lajoie's .422 that season was the sixth highest season average of all time. Few players ever dominated a season the way Lajoie did in 1901. He led the league not only in batting average, but also in hits, doubles, slugging, total bases, home runs, and runs batted in. Lajoie's 1901 slugging average of .635 was an American League record that stood for 18 years until it was broken by Babe Ruth. Wagner couldn't top those numbers (although Honus would say the American League wasn't exactly a major league during its first year in business).

Lajoie batted over .300 16 of his 21 years in the league. He did this despite playing in the Dead Ball era, when league averages were in the .230s and .240s. He led all batters in various categories 22 times over his career. He captured three batting crowns. How's this for a stretch: from 1899 to 1904, he hit .378, .337, .422, .366, .355, and .381 for a .373 average.

In 1904, Lajoie hit .381 when only six hitters in the entire league topped .300, so his .381 was amazing. It was 137 points above the league average. When Babe Ruth led the league with a .378 average in 1924, it was only 88 points above the league average. Thirty-seven players hit higher than .300 in 1924.

Lajoie's skills were admired so much when he was the player-manager for Cleveland that the team was known as the "Naps." Lajoie was popular all around the league, and that led to a scandal in 1910. As the season drew to a close, Lajoie and Ty Cobb were locked in a tight race for the batting title. The winner of the crown would get a highly prized Chalmers automobile.

On the last day of the season, Cobb was leading the race with a .385 average, so he decided to sit out the final game. Now, Cobb was as unpopular as Lajoie was popular, so when the Naps took the field for the first game of a double bill with the St. Louis Browns, the Browns players set out to help Lajoie win the title.

The Browns' third baseman deliberately played very deep, inviting Lajoie to bunt down the line for base hits. Nap took him up on the offer. In eight at bats, he got six hits, raising his average to .384. There was a dispute as to who won the title when some people said Cobb did not actually bat .385. The argument went back and forth for a week until the American League commissioner decided to award the title to Cobb.

Because it didn't like controversy, Chalmers stopped giving out cars to the batting title winners. Instead, the company awarded a car to the league's MVP. But because the company also admired Lajoie, both he and Cobb got cars in 1911.

More numbers

- Over the course of his career, he held or established some 70 batting records.
- Lajoie's career batting average is .338, 18th on the all-time list.
- He was first in slugging four times. He was in the top five in slugging eight times.
- He captured three RBI titles.
- Four times he led the league in hits.
- When he was 36 years old, he still hit .384 on a league-leading 227 hits.

The Rundown

HITS: His .422 in 1901 is still an American League record. He was a powerful hitter, who didn't hit many home runs in the Dead Ball era but instead adapted his stroke to smash frightening line drives. His batting averages were generally much higher than the rest of the league's. He had many seasons where he scored more than 100 runs or knocked in over 100 RBIs in a time when few runs were scored.

OUTS: His .422 in 1901 was accomplished during the first year of the American League when the competition wasn't as tough as it was in the National League. In that season, foul balls did not count as strikes. That also helped boost his average.

Ernie Lombardi.

ERNIE LOMBARDI

Nickname: Schnozz, Bocci
Given name: Ernesto Natali Lombardi
Born: April 6, 1908, Oakland, California
Died: September 26, 1977
Size: 6'3" 230 lbs.
Bats: right
Throws: right
Position: catcher
Career: 1931–1947

Almost everyone has an older, slow-moving uncle or grandfather, the kind of guy who spends most of his days in the La-Z-Boy dozing off in front of the TV. But here's the thing. That guy is probably a faster runner than Ernie Lombardi ever was. Ernie Lombardi spent most of his 17 years in the majors as a catcher with the Cincinnati Reds. He was big and slow. A turtle could have outrun him to first base. He was probably the slowest player to ever play in the major leagues.

But that's why he must have been one of the game's greatest hitters. Ernie hit .306 over his career. Ty Cobb hit .367, but how many of Cobb's hits were slow infield hits that he legged out for singles? Now, imagine how many slow-footed Ernie legged out; probably three. All his hits were of the power variety. No little nubbers from him.

With his 46-ounce bat, he hit the ball hard. How hard? Hall of Fame pitcher Carl Hubbell said Lombardi was the only hitter in the league who "truly frightened me, the only guy I thought might hurt me, might kill me."

Here's another reason why Ernie must have been one of the greatest. He was so slow and hit the ball so hard, the infielders played in the outfield and could still throw him out at first. At one point, Ernie told the Dodgers' Pee Wee Reese, "It was five years before I realized you were a short-stop."

Ernie was also famous for something else: people said he had the biggest nose of any player who ever lived. But there are no statistics for that.

Because he was so slow, people said he had to hit triples just to make a single. He must have done that a lot. In his best years, from 1935 to 1938, he hit .343, .333, .334, and in 1938, a league-leading .342.

Lombardi also had an incredible eye. The most he ever struck out in a season was 25 times. Compare that to Reggie Jackson, who struck out fewer than 100 times in a season only twice in his career.

The worst moment in his career came in Game 4 of the 1939 World Series. The Reds had already lost the first three games to the Yankees, but were winning 4–2 going into the ninth inning of Game 4 when the Bombers tied the score and sent the game into extra innings.

In the tenth with a man on third, Joe DiMaggio singled to center. Charlie Keller, known as "King Kong," raced home. The throw beat Keller, but King Kong hit Lombardi so hard it left the big catcher dazed on the ground, and the Yankees went on to win the Series. The next day's headlines read "The Schnozz's Great Snooze" and Lombardi was called "Sleeping Beauty," but the truth was several other Reds made errors that cost them the game. Ernie was just the victim of a hard hit. Still, people say he never got over the incident.

He was elected to the Hall of Fame in 1986. Evidently, the writers remembered what a great hitter he was.

More Numbers

- He was voted the MVP once.
- Ten times in his career he hit over .300.
- Lombardi played in four All-Star Games, hitting over .400.
- He once hit four doubles in four consecutive innings in a game against the Phillies.

The Rundown

HITS: He may have hit the ball harder than anyone, and despite his lack of speed, he still won two batting titles and one MVP award.

OUTS: Speed is an important aspect of hitting, and he had none.

Mickey Mantle.

MICKEY MANTLE

Nickname: The Commerce Comet, The Mick
Given name: Mickey Charles Mantle
Born: October 20, 1931, Spavinaw,
   Oklahoma
Died: August 13, 1995
Size: 5'11½" 195 lbs.
Bats: both left and right
Throws: right
Position: centerfield, first base
Career: 1951–1968

Mickey Mantle was crowned an American hero before he even arrived at Yankee Stadium in 1951. For the next 17 years he had to live up to that billing. Sometimes he did, and sometimes he didn't. But until the day he died, fans in and out of baseball worshipped Mantle like no other athlete since Babe Ruth. He could take their breath away with his tape-measure home runs or even his strikeouts.

Mickey Mantle had no choice but to be a great ballplayer. After all, he was named for Hall of Famer Mickey Cochrane. In 1951, Mantle arrived in Yankee Stadium from Commerce, Oklahoma, with enormous pressure on his shoulders. Joe DiMaggio, the game's greatest player, was a year from retirement, and the 19-year-old Mantle would replace him in centerfield.

At first he slumped. He was brought up too early. The pressure got to him. He was sent down to the minors for more seasoning. But the slump continued. He called his father on the phone and cried, "I don't think I can play baseball anymore."

The next day his dad barged into his hotel room. He threw Mantle's clothes into a suitcase. "You're going home. You'll work in the mines." Mickey knew he didn't want to do that, and he stopped feeling sorry for himself. Soon, he was on his way. He later said that incident with his father was the turning point of his life.

And what a job he did. If he hadn't injured his legs so often in his career, his numbers probably would have been the greatest of all. The physical problems started in high school when he developed a disease called osteomyelitis in his leg. That would trouble him the rest of his life. During his career, he had serious surgery on both knees, surgery for a broken foot, and surgery on his shoulder. And these were the days before arthroscopic surgery. Nowadays, with arthroscopic surgery, many times it only takes a few weeks to recover from an operation. In Mantle's time, surgeons could only do full surgery, and often it would take a year or more before a player was back to normal.

Reporters visiting the clubhouse for the first time were amazed at how much time Mantle had to spend wrapping his legs and making sure his knee braces stayed in place.

Still, when he arrived in New York, Mantle was known as "The Commerce Comet," the fastest player in the game. And maybe the strongest. The term "tape-measure home run" was invented after a publicist measured one of Mantle's blasts that flew clear out of Griffith Stadium in Washington, D.C. He estimated that it carried 565 feet.

Had it not been for the upper facade hanging over the rightfield stands, Mantle would have been the first to hit a fair ball out of Yankee Stadium during a major league game. The ball was still rising when it caromed off the facade 106 feet above the ground.

One day, a fan taunted the great Tigers star Al Kaline, "You're not half as good as Mickey Mantle." Kaline answered, "Son, nobody is half as good as Mickey Mantle."

Even though he was so quick, Mantle didn't steal a lot of bases. Stolen bases were less common in the '50s than other decades, because most hitters were looking to powder the ball. Hit-and-run baseball was as out of style as crew cuts were in the late 1960s. And with their powerful line-up, the Yankees did not have to look for the steal to score runs.

One indication of Mantle's speed is that while he had many RBIs, he scored more runs than he drove in (1,677 to 1,509). That means he circled the bases pretty quickly.

But what really made Mantle's batting feats so amazing was that he did them both left-handed and right-handed. He walloped 536 homers. Of those, he hit 373 from the left side and 163 from the right. No other switch-hitter has hit so many home runs.

While Hank Aaron hit 219 home runs more than Mantle, Mantle actually had a higher home run percentage than Aaron. It was higher than Willie Mays's, too. Two times he led the league in slugging and homers. But his greatest home run year was 1961 when he didn't win the home run crown. He and Roger Maris smashed everything in their path toward Babe Ruth's home run record of 60 in a season. Maris had the benefit of hitting in front of Mantle. He saw more fastballs from pitchers who didn't want to throw to the Mick. Then, typical of Mantle, he got hurt in the last month and missed too many games. Still, he finished with 54 homers to Maris's 61.

At his peak, he dominated the league the way Ted Williams and Ruth did at their best. From 1954 to 1961, he led the league in runs scored six times. And like Williams, pitchers were afraid of Mantle. He averaged over 100 walks a season because pitchers refused to throw him strikes.

When he was healthy, he also hit for average. He captured the Triple Crown in 1956 when he had one of the greatest seasons of all time. He hit .353, smashed 52 home runs, and drove home 130 runs. He won the Most Valuable Player award that year and then won it again in 1957 when he pushed his average up a notch to .365.

In 1962, his .605 slugging average led the league. He also batted .321, and even though he appeared in only 123 games, he won his third MVP. As one rival manager put it, "Mickey Mantle playing part-time is still better than anyone else in the league."

More Numbers

- He was a three-time MVP.
- He played on 16 All-Star teams.
- His career slugging average was .557.
- He led the league in runs scored six times.
- He was a four-time home run leader.

The Rundown

HITS: He was the greatest switch-hitter of all time and a three-time MVP and Triple Crown winner who hit enormous home runs and dominated the league in the 1950s. He drew a lot of walks because pitchers were afraid to pitch to him.

OUTS: He struck out a lot, and his lifetime average of .298 was low compared to the averages of many other great hitters. Because he swung for the fences so often, he didn't get as many RBIs as he should have. Over his 18-year career, he only had four seasons with more than 100 RBIs.

Willie Mays.

WILLIE MAYS

Nickname: Say Hey Kid
Given name: Willie Howard Mays
Born: May 6, 1931, Westfield, Alabama
Size: 5'10½" 170 lbs.
Bats: right
Throws: right
Position: centerfield
Career: 1951–1952, 1954–1973

They nicknamed Willie Mays the "Say Hey Kid" after the joyful way he greeted his friends and fans. That was also the exciting and infectious way he played baseball. Willie Mays was one of those players who could do everything. He could hit, hit for power, run, catch, and throw—all wonderfully. And if he didn't miss nearly two years for military service, it might have been his home run record that Hank Aaron was chasing in 1974.

As it was, Mays hit 660 lifetime home runs, good enough for third all time. He was so good, someone once said, "There are only two authentic geniuses, Willie Mays and Willie Shakespeare."

Just as it was with his rival Mickey Mantle, Mays had a tough introduction to the majors. Mays was hitting .477 for Minneapolis of the American Association when the 20-year-old was called up to play for the New York Giants in 1951. He promptly "stunk out the joint" as they say. After a few weeks, Mays was 0-for-26 and just beside himself.

"I'm hurting this team," he told his manager, Leo Durocher. "You'd better bench me or send me back to the minors."

"Don't worry," Durocher told him. "You're my center-fielder even if you don't get another hit for the rest of the year." Mays soon caught fire, and after the season he was named Rookie of the Year.

New Yorkers just loved the way Mays played the game. And when he wasn't smashing balls all over the Polo Grounds, local photographers frequently snapped him playing stickball out in the streets with the kids in his Harlem neighborhood.

No one had ever played baseball with such enthusiasm. And Willie could find all sorts of ways to win a game, whether it was with his arm, his feet, or his bat. In the 1954 World Series against the Cleveland Indians, he produced what may have been the single most electrifying play in baseball history. The Giants were underdogs against the Indians, who had won an American League record 111 games that year. But in the World Series, they had the starch knocked out of them in four straight by the Giants—in large part because of Mays.

The score was tied in the eighth inning of Game 1 when the Indians got two men on with no outs. Vic Wertz hit a line drive to the deepest part of centerfield in the Polo Grounds, 460 feet from home plate. Mays turned his back to the plate and out-raced the ball. He stuck out his mitt, grabbed the ball, and turned and threw it home in one motion. He not only made the out, but he also prevented the runner from scoring. Those who witnessed the play said they had never seen anything like it.

There wasn't anything Mays couldn't do. Babe Ruth could hit homers and hit for average, and he was a good base runner but not a great one. Cobb could steal and hit for average like no one else, but he never hit many home runs, even in the lively ball era of the 1920s.

Mays didn't hit for average the way Ruth or Cobb did, but he hit more homers than Cobb and was much faster than Ruth, and only he slammed 54 fewer round-trippers than Ruth did. Take into consideration the differences in the game between Ruth's and Mays's time, and that gap between the two narrows considerably.

In the 1950s, Mays had an excellent .317 average. That was 57 points higher than the rest of the league. In 1954, his .345 took the batting title. He also led the league in slugging with a .667 average. He would be tops in slugging five times.

But this was what made Mays so special: four straight years, from 1956 to 1959, he was the leading base thief in the league. He also led the league in triples for four years, from '54 to '57.

Mays produced a lot of runs during a time when not as many runs were scored. He scored over 100 runs in a season 12 years in a row, just one season behind the record held by Lou Gehrig and Hank Aaron. The season that broke the string, 1966, he scored 99. But over those 13 years, Mays outscored Aaron 1,520 to 1,461.

Mays didn't outscore Gehrig, but scoring totals in the '50s and '60s were much lower than they were in Gehrig's day. From 1930 to 1932, when Gehrig was at his run-scoring peak, the entire league scored 19,561 runs. From 1959 to 1961, the league scored 16,292. During those three years in the 1930s, Gehrig scored 444 runs or .023 percent of the league's runs. Mays, during his three years, scored 361 runs, but his total of the league's runs was .022. You can't get much closer than that.

Mays's RBI totals are also impressive. As we have seen, run totals were lower in Mays's day, but he still amassed over 100 RBIs eight years in a row. That ties the National League record with Mel Ott.

Those are pretty good numbers for a man who thought about quitting at first. Hall of Fame pitcher Warren Spahn remembered his role in helping Mays along. "He was something like 0-for-21 the first time I saw him. His first major league hit was a home run off me—and I'll never forgive myself," Spahn said. "We might have gotten rid of Willie forever if I'd only struck him out."

More Numbers

- On the all-time list, Mays is:
  - tenth in hits (3,283)
  - fourteenth in slugging average (.557)
  - third in total bases (6,066)
  - fourth in extra-base hits (1,323)
  - eighth in RBIs (1,903)
- He was the MVP twice, in 1954 and 1965, and played in every All-Star Game from 1954 to 1973.

The Rundown

HITS: What couldn't he do? He was the most exciting player of the 1950s and much of the '60s.

OUTS: Like Mantle, his lifetime batting average of .302 was lower than that of others. While his home run and RBI totals are among the best, he never led in RBIs. Others had higher home run and RBI percentages.

Mark McGwire.

MARK McGWIRE

Nickname: Big Mac
Given name: Mark David McGwire
Born: October 1, 1963, Pomona, California
Size: 6'5" 250 lbs.
Bats: right
Throws: right
Position: first base
Career: 1986–

Wow!
What else can you say about Mark McGwire's 1998 season. As a matter of fact, it was so amazing, we should say it again.

Wow! Even Babe Ruth and Ty Cobb would tip their caps to the man who not only set a new home run record, but did it by completely destroying the old one. Roger Maris set the record of 61 in 1961. He passed Ruth's mark by one, and he needed eight more games to do it. McGwire hit his 62nd home run of the season in his 145th game. After 154 games, McGwire had 63.

Even McGwire was amazed. "It's unheard of for someone to hit 70 home runs," he said. "I can't believe I did it. It blows me away."

Look at it this way to see how amazing it was. Seventy homers is a 15 percent increase over 61 homers. The highest recorded batting average for a season in the modern age is Rogers Hornsby's .424. If someone were to beat that by 15 percent he would have to hit .488. That is simply not going to happen.

Hack Wilson holds the single-season record for RBIs with 190. To beat that by 15 percent, some kind of superhuman would have to send home 219 runs.

Actually McGwire did even better than these numbers show. He should have been credited with 71 homers. A terrible call by an umpire, who thought he saw fan interference (the replays proved him wrong) on one ball that had cleared the fence, should have been another home run.

And here is something else amazing about his 1998 season: when he hit 65 in 1999, it was about as exciting as an infield fly. By then, breaking 60 was no big deal. So who is this guy who stands at home plate as big as a moving van and as dangerous as a bull who got up too early that morning? It was said of Ted Williams that his eyesight was so sharp, he could read the label of a spinning record. McGwire's eyesight is so bad that he could hardly read the disk if it was sitting still right in front of his face. He has to wear contact lenses to see the pitcher. His biggest hero is his father, who is a dentist but was previously a boxer, even though a childhood illness left one leg much shorter than the other. Mark's dad just worked and worked until he succeeded.

Mark is the same way. He works out in the gym every day. He has had many injuries over the years that have forced him to miss hundreds of games, but that has only made him work harder to get into shape. "Things happen for a reason," McGwire said. "Hard work pays off." His high school coach agreed. "Mark was not afraid to work," said Tom Carroll. "God gave him talent, but he worked hard, and that set him apart."

McGwire always wanted to be a pitcher when he was young. But a home run that he hit in his first Little League game at 10 years old showed that he might be more valuable at the plate.

Twelve years later, he served notice on the rest of the league in his rookie season with Oakland when he hit 49 home runs to shatter the rookie record of 39.

McGwire missed nearly the whole 1993 and 1994 seasons with a bad heel and a good part of 1995 with a bad back. He thought of quitting, but he remembered how hard his dad had worked after his illness. So after a couple of operations, he put in many extra hours in the weight room and came back stronger than ever. Even though he had only 317 at bats in

1995, he still hit 39 home runs. That means he hit a homer in every 8.13 at bats. Until 1998 when he averaged 7.27, that was the best percentage in the history of the game.

So has McGwire surpassed Ruth and Aaron as the greatest home run hitting machine of all time? Maybe. He is still playing, so he doesn't yet have their lifetime home run numbers. But let's look at some other figures. Ruth averaged a home run every 11.76 at bats. Aaron averaged a home run every 16.4 at bats. McGwire averages a home run every 10.63 at bats. That's the best average of all time.

And when it comes to a single-season home run average, McGwire not only holds first place but also second, third, and fourth. Finally, in fifth, is Babe Ruth, who hit a home run in every 8.48 at bats in 1920. The year he hit 60 homers, his average was 9.00.

And McGwire didn't just hit 70 balls over the fence, but his four-baggers averaged over 420 feet. There are no statistics indicating whether that is a record, but there are no indications that any other player, Ruth included, hit them consistently farther.

McGwire's 52 homers in 1996; 58 in 1997; 70 in 1998; and 65 in 1999 broke his own record for consecutive seasons of more than 50 homers. His total of four 50 home run seasons ties a record previously held alone by Babe Ruth. McGwire might have had 50 in 1987, but he cut his season short with 49 so he could be with his wife when his son was born.

Needless to say, his 245 homers from '96 to '99 are the highest ever for a four-year period. Imagine: he averaged 61 over those seasons!

McGwire is not just a home run hitter. His 1998 slugging average of .752 was the highest season total in the National League since Rogers Hornsby's .756 in 1925. He has driven home more than 100 RBIs in a season seven times and led the league with 147 in 1999. In 1998, he also set a National League record for walks in a season with 162. Think of how many homers he would have hit if pitchers had put the ball near the plate. All those walks helped give him an on-base percentage in 1998 of .470. Clearly, pitchers were scared to death of him. For good reason.

More Numbers

• He reached 400 as well as 500 home runs with fewer at bats than any other player.

The Rundown

HITS: Let's face it, he's from another world when it comes to home runs. His season home run totals and averages are simply the best of all time.

OUTS: But let's put the record in some context. Behind McGwire was Sammy Sosa, who also destroyed Maris's record with 66 home runs. In 1998, four players had more than 50 home runs (and Albert Belle came close with 49). That's a record. It also makes McGwire's 70 seem less dominating than, let's say, Babe Ruth's total of 54 in 1920 when the second highest total was George Kelly's 11. The Introduction lists several reasons why offensive numbers were juiced in the '90s. Also, while McGwire's single-season home run marks are better than Ruth's, his lifetime slugging and RBI numbers are not even close. Neither is his lifetime batting average. What he does is hit home runs. The Cardinals were a poor team in 1998 and 1999, finishing well out of playoff contention. That suggests that home run hitting can be overrated.

Stan Musial.

STAN MUSIAL

Nickname: Stan the Man
Given name: Stanley Frank Musial
Born: November 21, 1920, Donora,
　　　　Pennsylvania
Size: 6' 175 lbs.
Bats: left
Throws: left
Position: leftfield
Career: 1941–1944, 1946–1963

They called Stan Musial "The Man," and for 22 years in St. Louis he was. There have been few athletes more beloved in their hometown than Musial. He took his class act not only on the field but off it as well.

And what a player he was! Musial bridged the era between the old game of the '30s and '40s to the modern era. During that time, he captured seven batting championships and six slugging crowns, and led five times in runs scored and twice in RBIs.

And none of it would have happened had it not been for an accident that occurred in 1940. That year, Musial was a rookie minor league pitcher. He was 18-5 and had a bright future as a major league hurler. But one day when he dove for a line drive, he hurt his pitching shoulder. A lump formed, and he couldn't pitch again.

The Cards knew the 19-year-old kid had a pretty sharp batting eye, so they made him into an outfielder. Good move. His lifetime batting average is .331, 24th all time. Only Ted Williams and Tony Gwynn have higher lifetime averages from the modern era.

Musial had a funny batting stance. A left-handed hitter, he would stand in the back of the box coiled in a crouch. Hall of Fame pitcher Ted Lyons said he looked like "a small boy looking around a corner to see if the cops are coming."

Clearly it worked. Musial is fourth in total hits with 3,630. Of the three ahead of him only Ty Cobb had a higher batting average. Musial lashed 976 more hits than Williams.

He hit many fewer home runs than Aaron, but had more doubles and triples. His batting average was also 26 points higher than Aaron's. With the exception of the in-the-park home run, a triple might be the hardest hit to come by in baseball. It requires both power and speed. Musial's 177 triples are the most of the modern era.

Joe Garagiola was a catcher with the Pirates, and he often played against Musial. "Stan comes sauntering up to the plate and asks me how my family's making out," Garagiola said. "Before I can answer him, he's on third base."

Musial had 1,377 extra-base hits, trailing only Aaron, who had 1,477, but remember Aaron had nearly 1,400 more at bats than Musial.

Musial also hit for power. He hit 475 home runs in his career and led the league in slugging average six times. His .559 slugging average is ninth best all time for players who have finished their careers, directly in front of Mays, Mantle, Aaron, and the great home run hitter Ralph Kiner.

He once hit three home runs in the first game of a double-header and two in the second game.

The most important thing a batter can do is produce runs. Baseball history is full of players who have high batting averages but don't score or produce many runs. Musial was the opposite. He was one of the great run producers of all time. Five times he led the league in runs scored, and 11 times had over 100 runs scored in a season. Twice he led the league in RBIs, and 10 times had over 100 RBIs in a season.

He had so many terrific years, but 1948 really stands out as one of the best seasons that any player has ever had. His .376 average led the league. He also led in RBIs, runs, doubles, triples, on-base percentage, total hits, and slugging.

Ralph Kiner and Johnny Mize both hit 40 homers that year to prevent Musial from capturing the Triple Crown. Needless to say, he won the MVP that year.

"No man has ever been a perfect ballplayer," said Ty Cobb in the 1950s. "Stan Musial, however, is the closest thing to perfection in the game today." The pitcher Warren Spahn agreed. "He's the only batter I ever intentionally walked with the bases loaded."

The people who saw him play thought a lot of him during his career. He won the MVP three times. Four times he was second and was in the top five nine times. He was named to the *Sporting News* All-Star team 12 times. According to baseball statistician Bill James, Musial did better in MVP voting than any other player.

There was something else about Musial that made him special. In 1947, Jackie Robinson became the first black man to play in the modern major leagues (there were blacks who played in the nineteenth century). Many white players were deeply unhappy, and outside of his own teammates, Robinson had hardly a friend around the league. On the Cardinals, there was talk of a strike if Robinson was allowed to play. Word got back to Musial and he would have none of it.

That year, the Cardinals treated Robinson brutally. The worst incident occurred when Enos Slaughter deliberately spiked Robinson in a play at first base. The next inning, when they met at first base, Robinson told Musial what he really would like to do to Slaughter and his teammates.

"I don't blame you," Musial told him.

That's another reason why they called him "The Man."

More Numbers

- He won seven batting titles.
- He is third in doubles (725).
- He slugged .600 or better six times.
- He led the National League in total bases six times.

- He led the National League in hits six times.
- He led the National League in doubles eight times.
- He led the National League in triples five times.

The Rundown

HITS: He hit for average and hit for power. He had an extra-ordinary number of extra-base hits.

OUTS: Others had a higher home run percentage.

Babe Ruth.

BABE RUTH

Nicknames: Babe, the Bambino, the Sultan of Swat

Given name: George Herman Ruth

Born: February 6, 1895, Baltimore, Maryland

Died: August 16, 1948

Size: 6'2" 215 lbs.

Bats: left

Throws: left

Position: rightfield, pitcher

Career: 1914–1935

f there was any one player who might have been bigger than baseball, it was Babe Ruth. How big a star was he? This big: during the battle of Guadalcanal in World War II, Japanese soldiers tried to get American GIs angry by yelling at them, "To hell with Babe Ruth."

Ruth was such a huge star they had to invent a new word to describe his incredible feats. The word was "Ruthian." What else could it be? Yet, if you watch the old newsreels of the Babe, you'll see a fellow with a potbelly circling the bases in little steps, and you'll wonder what all the fuss was about.

What it was about was this man who set so many records and dominated the game in so many ways, there really was no better term than Ruthian.

"He hit the ball harder and farther than any man I ever saw," said Bill Dickey, who played with Ruth and Gehrig, and saw Mantle, Williams, Aaron, and Mays when they were in their prime.

The Babe burst on the national scene, hitting more home runs than anybody had ever imagined. He became America's biggest star in the Roaring '20s when people like Charles Lindbergh, Jack Dempsey, and Red Grange captured the country's imagination.

Nobody had ever seen anyone like him. He could drive faster, party longer, drink more, and eat more than anyone. He wasn't human, some people said. "Born? Hell, Babe

Ruth wasn't born. He fell from a tree," laughed his teammate Joe Dugan.

Ruth seemed to be bigger than life. Sportswriter Bob Broeg said of him, "To try to capture Babe Ruth with cold statistics would be like trying to keep up with him on a night out."

Ruth was raised in a reform school and knew precious little about basic manners. When he signed his first professional contract at 19, he was really an overgrown kid, a "Babe," his teammates on the Baltimore Orioles called him. They liked to tell stories of his huge appetite. He was known to drink six bottles of soda along with a snack before going to bed. One player recalled his eating a breakfast of an omelet made with 18 eggs, six slices of toast, and three big slices of ham, washed down with a few cups of coffee.

Ruth's biographer Robert Creamer recorded another legendary dinner that had him eating an entire chicken, potatoes, spinach, corn, peas, beans, bread, butter, pie, ice cream, and three or four cups of coffee.

All that food didn't hurt him at the plate. Ruth was one of the most feared batters in history—and for good reason. He had enormous strength, and he swung at the ball with a natural uppercut that sent the ball out in enormous arcs. He didn't hit line drives like Joe Jackson or Lou Gehrig did, he hit moon shots.

One day in 1919, he smashed a ball so high and so far, a sportswriter who saw it said when it came down it had ice on it. Another sportswriter who was there, Fred Leib, went out and measured the distance that it traveled and couldn't believe his eyes when it came out to 625 feet.

Ruth swung a thick 42-ounce bat that looked like a tree trunk in comparison to the bats other players used. And unlike most of the other hitters of the Dead Ball era, he wasn't looking to place the ball. He placed his hands at the bottom of the barrel and swung as hard as he could. Sometimes, he'd swing and miss so hard, his body would corkscrew into a complete circle. He led the league in strikeouts five times, although he never struck out 100 times in a season, which is common among today's sluggers.

Ruth said he benefited from his hard swing. "I swing as hard as I can, and I try to swing right through the ball. The harder you grip the bat, the more you can swing it through the ball, and the farther the ball will go. I swing big, with everything I've got."

Ruth may have swung hard, but one teammate said Ruth had "the prettiest swing" he ever saw. And even though his bat was big, Ruth was so strong and his hands so quick he could wait for the last second before deciding whether the pitch was a fastball or a curve and then lash out at the ball and drive it over the fence.

Ruth liked to stroll up to the plate, nice and slow. He would joke with the umpires and take just enough time to build tension with the fans and the other players. Sometimes he would laugh at the pitcher after he smacked a homer. Then he would circle the bases and make sure to tip his hat to the crowd before disappearing into the dugout.

He was also a fearless hitter. Hitting can be dangerous, and the fear of getting hit by a pitched ball is one of the toughest things for a hitter to overcome. When you see a hitter duck away from a curve, you know he has that fear inside him, and that's what keeps many averages down. Pitchers know this, and that's why they often come way inside with a pitch and push the hitter back from the plate. Once they succeed in doing that, they can easily drop a pitch on the outside corner for a strike.

The manager Casey Stengel recalled that Ruth could hardly ever be driven away from the plate. "He was very brave. You never saw him fall away from a pitch," Stengel said.

When you consider Ruth's amazing batting statistics, remember this: he only batted 678 times the first five years of his career because he was primarily a pitcher—and a Ruthian one at that. Twice he won over 20 games. His lifetime earned run average is 2.28.

But this is a book about offense, so let's look at his astounding numbers at the plate. The Babe was still a pitcher in his second year in the league when he first made his mark as a slugger. The home run champ that year was Braggo Roth with seven in 384 at bats. Ruth socked four in 92 at bats.

By 1918, he was proving to be such a great hitter that his manager had him split his time between pitching and the outfield. That year he tied Tilly Walker for the home run crown with 11. Walker had 414 at bats; the Babe, just 317.

There wasn't anyone even close next year when he demolished the competition with 29 home runs. Walker was second with 10. That means Ruth almost tripled his number. Let's jump ahead to 1998 for a second when Sammy Sosa hit 66 home runs. If Mark McGwire had tripled that, he would have hit 198!

Ruth's 29 four-baggers were more than entire teams hit. Only the Yankees as a team had more home runs than Ruth did alone.

In 1920, Ruth was sold to the Yanks for $100,000 in cash and a $300,000 loan because Red Sox owner Harry Frazee needed money to produce a Broadway show. Eighty years later, Red Sox fans still haven't forgiven him.

What the Babe accomplished in 1920 and 1921 was Ruthian even for him. Playing full-time in the outfield, he smacked 54 round-trippers in 1920. How overwhelming was that? George Sisler was next with 19. The home run champ in the National League that year was Cy Williams with 15.

In 1921, he broke his own home run record when he smashed 59 four-baggers. Second was Ken Williams with 24. He also led the league in total bases, runs, RBIs, and walks. His .378 average was third behind Harry Heilmann and Ty Cobb.

Ruth would lead the American League in home runs 12 times. There were only five seasons in his 15 as a full-time player that he didn't win the title. He missed another home run crown by four homers in 1922 only because he was suspended for six weeks for playing pro ball in the off-season.

He was the first player to hit 30, 40, 50, and 60 home runs in a season. Four times he walloped over 50 home runs in a season. Aaron never once hit 50. Mark McGwire is the only other player to do it four times.

Ruth's record of 60 home runs stood for 34 years until it was broken by Roger Maris. When Ruth hit his 700th home run in 1934, no other ballplayer had even hit 300. His record of 714 lifetime home runs stood until Aaron broke it in 1974. Aaron would stop at 755, but he also had nearly 4,000 more at bats than Ruth did. Several hundred of those at bats were as a DH. Ruth didn't have that luxury. Ruth could only come to the plate if he played the field.

He also set a record for slugging in 1920 that still stands at .847. In 1921, Ruth's .846 slugging average nearly broke his own record. George Sisler finished second in slugging, over 200 points behind. No one before or since has ever led those categories by such margins. No hitter has ever come within 75 points of Ruth's slugging record.

Ruth's lifetime slugging average of .690 is 21 points higher than Aaron's best season. The second highest lifetime is Ted Williams, at a distant .634. McGwire is at .593, and that figure is bound to go down as his career fades.

Hank Aaron owns the major league record for most RBIs in a career with 2,297. Ruth is second with 2,211, but while Ruth's percentage of RBIs per game is fifth best lifetime, Aaron's is only 25th.

Ruth also hit for average. His best was .393 in 1923. The next year he took the AL batting crown, hitting .378.

He did pretty well in World Series play too. He hit .326 over 10 World Series with a slugging average of .744. That's second to Reggie Jackson's .755, although Ruth played in twice as many World Series as Reggie did.

Ruth's most famous moment in World Series play was in Game 3 of the 1932 Fall Classic. He had been taking a lot of insults from the Cubs players, At one point they rolled a lemon out on the field when he came up to hit in the first inning. The story goes that Ruth became so angry he told the Chicago bench he was going to hit a home run off their pitcher Charlie Root.

Old black-and-white film does show Ruth gesturing just before he blasted a pitch into the right centerfield bleachers. Whether he "called his shot" as later sportswriters said, we'll never know, but Ruth said he did. Would anyone else have been capable of such a Ruthian effort?

More Numbers

- In seven of the 12 years in which Ruth led the American League in home runs, he also had the most in both leagues.
- His home run percentage of 8.5 is still the highest of all time. His .342 lifetime batting average is tied for 11th on the list. He hit over .300 17 times. He eclipsed .370 six times.
- He won six RBI crowns and drove in over 100 RBIs 13 times. Five times he drove in over 150 runs.
- Ruth led the league in slugging a record 13 times.
- He led the league in walks 11 times.
- Ruth's 457 total bases in 1921 are still a major league record.
- He also led the league in runs scored eight times. He is second to Ty Cobb in lifetime runs scored.
- Ruth's 177 runs scored in 1921 has never been topped in the modern era.
- Ruth even set a record for setting records—192 during his career.

The Rundown

HITS: He had the game's most outstanding power numbers for both home runs and slugging. He completely dominated in home runs, slugging, RBIs, and runs scored. He also hit for average.

OUTS: He led the league in strikeouts four times.

Al Simmons.

AL SIMMONS

Nickname: Bucketfoot Al
Given name: Aloysius Harry Szymanski
Born: May 22, 1902, Milwaukee, Wisconsin
Died: May 26, 1956
Size: 5'11" 190 lbs.
Bats: right
Throws: right
Position: centerfield
Career: 1924–1941, 1943–1944

A l Simmons's real name was Aloysius Harry Szymanski. That didn't sound like a Hall of Fame hitter. Besides, nobody could pronounce it. Then one day he saw a billboard in Milwaukee advertising the Simmons hardware company, and Aloysius Harry Szymanski was no more.

In the majors, they called him "Bucketfoot Al" because of his odd batting stance. And what a strange way of hitting it was. Simmons was a right-handed batter, but as he faced the pitcher he pulled his left foot all the way to the side so that it was basically facing third base. People laughed, but his manager Connie Mack said, "If he can hit, I don't care if he stands on his head."

He did hit. Simmons bettered .300 the first 11 years of his career, averaging .364. He topped .380 four times.

He was one of the big reasons why the Philadelphia Athletics of the late '20s were one of the greatest teams of all time, if not the greatest. But Simmons almost didn't play for the A's. When he was young, he wrote a letter to the Giants organization, informing them he was available. He never heard back, so instead he signed with the A's.

"Can you imagine what I'd have hit in the Polo Grounds with those short fences?" Simmons later asked. It was true. Simmons was a line drive hitter who would have had a field day in the Giants' park with its leftfield fences that were 280 feet down the line. In Shibe Park, where Simmons played his best years, he had to hit the ball 335 feet in left to reach the fence.

Simmons was one of the first real students of hitting. He would spend hours watching movies of himself. Another reason for his great success was his anger. Simmons was big and tough and just plain mean. "I was a fighting, snarling player on the field," he said. "I am proud, not ashamed of that reputation." Another time he said, "Pitchers, I want them dead."

Simmons was nearly six feet tall and tough as old leather. On Memorial Day in 1930, the team played a doubleheader. Simmons homered to tie the score of the opener in the ninth inning. In the 13th inning, Simmons rounded third base with the winning run, but before he got to home his knee popped. It turned out a blood vessel had burst. Simmons was told he had to go to the hospital immediately. He refused. Instead, he kept his uniform on in case he was needed in the nightcap. He was. In the fourth inning, he came up with the bases loaded and smashed a grand slam that propelled the team to victory.

After that season, a rival manager checked Simmons's stats and found out he had hit 14 homers in the eighth or ninth inning. Each one figured in the outcome of the game. "With men on base, Jimmie Foxx can be a pain, but Simmons is a plague," said Hall of Fame pitcher Red Ruffing.

The numbers bear him out. Simmons topped 100 RBIs in 12 of his first 13 years. In his first 11 years, he averaged 125 RBIs a season. Maybe that's lower than Lou Gehrig's average, but Simmons didn't have Ruth hitting in front of him like Gehrig did. Simmons batted .329 in four World Series. His lifetime World Series slugging average of .658 is fifth all time. Against the best, he was among the best, hitting .462 in three All-Star Games, and the game wasn't even played until he was past his prime.

At his peak, Simmons always seemed to be among the league leaders in hitting. Twice he lost the batting title on the last day of the season to Harry Heilmann. In 1930, he edged out Lou Gehrig for the batting crown, hitting .381 to Gehrig's .379. That season, he led the league in runs scored with 152, and his 165 RBIs were second to Gehrig. He was also third in slugging average, fifth in homers, and fourth in triples.

"A man is never a real champion unless he repeats," Simmons was told, so he repeated. He won the title again in 1931, this time hitting .390. Second place was Babe Ruth with a .373 average.

But already Simmons was suffering from rheumatism in his ankles, and he was never the same again even though he hit over .300 five more times in his career.

Five years in a row he had 200 or more hits. Even Cobb never had five consecutive 200-hit seasons. No American Leaguer would do it again until Wade Boggs. But he was a much more powerful hitter than Boggs, with 307 homers in his career.

In the all-important category of producing runs, he was one of the greatest.

How did the people who saw him play regard him? Six times he was named to the *Sporting News* All-Star team. In 1929, the Athletics murdered the Yankees' great Murderers Row by 18 games. Philadelphia had five future Hall of Famers. That year, Al Simmons was named the league's MVP by the *Sporting News*.

More Numbers

- His 253 hits in 1925 are the fourth highest ever.
- Simmons's .334 career average is 20th all time.
- He slugged over .500 10 times, had three seasons over .600, and reached .708 in 1930.

The Rundown

HITS: Simmons was a clutch performer who hit for average but, more important, drove in runs. And when it especially counted, in World Series play, he was terrific.

OUTS: Because he played at a time when averages were higher, he only led the league in major batting categories eight times.

George Sisler.

GEORGE SISLER

Nickname: Gorgeous George
Given name: George Harold Sisler
Born: March 24, 1893, Manchester, Ohio
Died: March 26, 1973
Size: 5'11" 170 lbs.
Bats: left
Throws: left
Position: first base
Career: 1915–1922, 1924–1930

Babe Ruth, Lou Gehrig, Ty Cobb, Ted Williams, George Sisler.

George Sisler? Who's that? You'd better find out, because at his peak, he may have been as good as all of them.

Like Ruth, Sisler arrived on the big league scene as a pitcher. He was discovered by Branch Rickey, who would bring Jackie Robinson into professional baseball some 30 years later. Rickey spotted Sisler at a practice game at the University of Michigan. Sisler was a freshman, and Rickey watched as he mowed down one varsity hitter after another. He struck out 20 of 21 varsity batters that faced him.

A little while later, Rickey was named general manager of the St. Louis Browns. One of the first calls he made was to Sisler, and he offered him a contract. Sisler signed and became such a good pitcher that he even beat the great Walter Johnson in a game. But, like Ruth, his bat was even better, so Sisler became a first baseman. And if it wasn't for an illness that dulled his eyesight, he might have had the best numbers of all.

If you doubt it, check out Gorgeous George's gorgeous numbers in 1920. He played in every inning of every game of the 154-game season. His .407 average led the league. He had 257 hits. That's still a major league record for a single season.

Two years later, he pushed his average even higher, to .420. Only Rogers Hornsby had a higher single-season average in the modern era. Not only are his 257 hits first on the all-time list for a single season, his 246 in 1922 are eighth. He is the only player who made the top 10 list for hits in a season twice. No wonder Ty Cobb called Sisler "the perfect ballplayer."

Many averages went up in 1920 for reasons listed in the Introduction. Sisler's did as well. But he was already among the top hitters in baseball. From 1917 to 1919, he hit .353, .341, and .342 for second, third, and third in the batting race. He was also in the top five in slugging for each of those years. And that was before he reached his prime.

Then Sisler missed the entire 1923 season with a severe sinus infection, and after that he was never the same. Bill James, who is regarded as one of baseball's leading historians, uses math to rate players. It is his guess that if Sisler hadn't got sick, he might have had 4,000 hits in his career. Imagine, even with eyes that were damaged by illness, he still managed to reach 200 hits a season three more times.

Although this is a book about hitting, it's almost impossible to talk about Sisler without mentioning that he was also one of the greatest fielding first basemen of all time. How good? Here's one example. In a game against the Yankees, one of the Bombers hit a grounder wide of first. Sisler moved in and grabbed the ball and lobbed it over to the pitcher covering the bag. Only the pitcher wasn't there. When Sisler saw this, he darted over to the bag, and caught his own throw to beat the runner!

More Numbers

- He smacked over 200 hits in a season six times.
- His 719 hits from 1920 to 1922 are the highest ever recorded over three consecutive seasons.
- He hit safely in 41 consecutive games in 1922, an American League record until it was broken by Joe DiMaggio in 1941.

The Rundown

HITS: At his peak, he hit for average almost as well as anyone. If you had to pick the greatest hitter based on his greatest season, you'd have to consider the year he had in 1920.

OUTS: Because of illness, he didn't have sustained greatness in RBIs or runs scored. He had little power.

Tris Speaker.

TRIS SPEAKER

Nicknames: Spoke, The Gray Eagle
Given name: Tristram E. Speaker
Born: April 4, 1888, Hubbard, Texas
Died: December 8, 1958
Size: 5′11½″ 193 lbs.
Bats: left
Throws: left
Position: centerfield
Career: 1907–1928

J ust a few pages ago, we mentioned George Sisler's ability at first base. But you can't do that without talking about the amazing feats of Tris Speaker in centerfield. Speaker would play almost directly behind second base and dare the batter to hit one over his head. The hitter would take him up on it, but almost always Spoke would track the ball down.

It wasn't unusual for him to catch a line drive in front of him and then step on second for a double play. With Tris out there, it was like having an extra infielder. Nobody ever played center that way or that well.

But in some ways that is Speaker's problem. He was such a terrific fielder, few people remember what a great hitter he was. There wasn't a better doubles hitter in the history of the game. He led the league in two-baggers eight times. His 792 doubles are number one all time. He smashed 50 or more doubles in a season five times. Ty Cobb never hit 50 doubles in a season. Neither did Ruth or Williams. Gehrig did it once.

As for triples, the great test of strength and speed, his 223 are sixth, with only Cobb and Sam Crawford ahead of him from his era.

In the Dead Ball era, Speaker had power and actually tied for the league lead in home runs with 10 in 1912. He had speed, with 433 lifetime stolen bases, and he also hit for average. When Ty Cobb won nine straight batting championships and was driving for a tenth, one man prevented him—Tris Speaker. That year, 1916, Speaker captured the crown by hitting .386 to Cobb's .371.

Speaker hit out of a crouch with the bat held low at his hip, and he would wiggle it nervously as he waited for the pitch. Spoke would hit .380 or higher five times and over .350 nine times. When he was 35, he hit .380, led the league in doubles for the eighth time, and smacked 218 hits. Cobb was 31 when he last had as many as 218 hits.

When he was 37 years old in 1925, Speaker hit .389. He was just five hits shy of .400. Speaker may or may not have been the greatest hitter of all time, but when it comes to hitting and defense, there can be no doubt that no other player succeeded so well at both.

More Numbers

• His .345 lifetime average is tied for seventh all time.
• He topped .300 18 of his 22 years in the majors.
• Speaker's 3,514 hits are fifth all time.
• He scored more than 100 runs in a season seven times.
• His 1,881 runs are ninth all time.

The Rundown

HITS: He hit for average and had line drive power along with excellent speed. He was still an exceptional hitter at the end of his long career.

OUTS: For the most part, whatever he did well at the plate, Ty Cobb did a little better. He did not have a lot of home run power.

Bill Terry.

🟠 BILL TERRY

Nickname: Memphis Bill
Given name: William Harold Terry
Born: October 30, 1896, Atlanta, Georgia
Died: January 9, 1989
Size: 6'1" 200 lbs.
Bats: left
Throws: left
Position: first base
Career: 1923–1936

Quick, who was the last player to hit over .400 in the majors? Most fans know the answer to that—Ted Williams. But who was the last National League player to surpass that magic mark?

Okay, you probably can figure out the answer. It was in 1930 when Terry hit .401. Like Al Simmons, Terry was an angry ballplayer. He came from a broken home in Jacksonville, Florida. He took the rage from his childhood experiences and channeled it into pummeling line drives. Baseball was a business to Terry, not pleasure. When he was elected to the Hall of Fame in 1954, all he could say was "I have nothing to say about it."

He feasted on the Polo Grounds' deep power alleys, especially in left centerfield. While he was a powerful hitter, he rarely tried to pull the ball. Instead, he averaged more than 37 doubles a year in what was basically 10 full years in the league. Tris Speaker, who holds the major league record for lifetime doubles with 792, averaged 40 a year.

Terry was also a hit machine. From 1929 to 1935, he failed to make 200 hits only once, averaging 212 a year. During Cobb's best seven years, he averaged 208 hits a season. In Hornsby's best seven years, he averaged 209.

Terry's lifetime .341 average is second only to Rogers Hornsby's in the National League. But he didn't just hit for average. From 1927 to 1932, he drove in over 100 runs every season. He also scored over 100 runs in a season six years in a row in that same span. The best Cobb did was four in a row.

More Numbers

• His 254 hits in 1930 are the second highest ever recorded in a single season, tying Lefty O'Doul for the National League record.

The Rundown

HITS: He was the National League's last .400 hitter, a real line drive machine with six seasons of over 200 hits.

OUTS: He didn't hit with a lot of power. He only had 154 homers. His .400 season came in a year when the National League average was a very high .303.

Frank Thomas.

FRANK THOMAS

Nickname: The Big Hurt
Given name: Frank Edward Thomas
Born: May 27, 1968, Columbus, Georgia
Size: 6'5" 270 lbs.
Bats: right
Throws: right
Position: first base, DH
Career: 1990–

Imagine what a pitcher must be thinking when Frank Thomas strolls up to the plate. First of all, Thomas is huge, so the poor pitcher must be wondering if he might be killed by a line drive. And if the pitcher doesn't get knocked out of the box, there's the danger of his getting knocked out of the game, because Thomas not only hits for power but has one of the highest lifetime averages among all current players. And then, if the pitcher says, "Well, I'll try to strike him out," he can forget about that, because not only does he hit for power and for average, he hardly ever gets K'd. His best hope might be to get a petition going and have him declared illegal.

Pitchers, more than anyone else, know why they call Frank Thomas "The Big Hurt." But it's also a way to describe the sadness in this big man's early life. But without those setbacks, Thomas may not have gotten where he is today.

When Frank was a boy, he loved his baby sister more than anything in the world. She was sickly, and it was his job to look after her. She died of leukemia when he was nine. Soon after she died, Frank announced that in her honor he was going to be a great baseball player one day. He worked hard at it. And if someone told him he couldn't do something he did it anyway. Like when he was cut the first year he went out for his high school baseball team. The next year he hit .472 and led the team to its first state championship.

When he graduated, no baseball team drafted him. He was so big, they thought he would be a football player. He did play one season as a tight end for the Auburn Tigers, but then he quit to play baseball. Even though he hit .385, he still didn't make the U.S. Olympic team, so he worked harder. The White Sox signed him, and he played a season in the minors before they invited him to spring training in 1990. He had a great spring, but still the team sent him down.

That made him angry. He took it out on the minor league pitchers until the Sox had to bring him up. Thomas finally proved them all wrong for good when he hit .330 the rest of the season.

"Those were the three most down days in my boy's life," said his father. "The day we lost my baby girl, the day nobody drafted him, and the day he didn't get to stay up."

Now, nobody doubts he is one of baseball's top hitters. What's the best way to pitch to him? "Throw it 10 feet in front of home plate and hope he doesn't hit it on a hop," says Buck Showalter, the manager of the Arizona Diamondbacks.

"I wish they'd let us put on the mask and shin guards," said pitcher Dennis Martinez. "Pitchers shouldn't be left out there alone with him."

Here's why not.

Thomas is the only player in major league history to record a .300 batting average, with 20 home runs, 100 RBIs, 100 runs scored, and 100 walks seven years in a row.

Even in 1998 when his batting average dipped below .300 for the first time, he still scored over 100 runs and drove home 109 to go along with his 29 four-baggers. After struggling again in 1999, he had a great comeback year in 2000 with a .328 average, 43 homers, and 143 RBIs.

After 10 seasons, his career slugging average is .573. That's ninth all time. Among current players, he is tied with Albert Belle; only Mark McGwire is better with a .587 average.

Thomas's lifetime batting average is .321, third among active players behind Tony Gwynn and Mike Piazza. But

Gwynn is not in the same ballpark—the same country even—in terms of power. Thomas has 344 lifetime homers and 1,183 RBIs. Gwynn has 134 home runs and 1,121 RBIs, but he also has nearly twice the number of at bats Thomas has.

If you're comparing Thomas against Griffey, forget about it. The only category that Griffey has better numbers than Thomas is home runs. Otherwise, Thomas outhits him and outslugs him. In most categories, it's the same against McGwire.

Thomas's RBIs per game is .77, just ahead of McGwire. Among those who played after World War II, only Joe DiMaggio and Ted Williams are higher.

If you measure a hitter by the number of times he gets on base, there aren't too many who are better in that category either. He's an extraordinarily patient hitter, who knows the value of taking his pitch. If he doesn't get it, he'll take the walk. Only once in his career has Thomas had an on-base percentage lower than .400—in 1998 when it was .381.

Thomas's lifetime on-base percentage is .440. Let's look at some of the other great hitters. Willie Mays's is .383; Henry Aaron's .373; Mickey Mantle's .420; Joe DiMaggio's .398; Ty Cobb's .423; Lou Gehrig's .442. Only Ted Williams and Babe Ruth were higher, and it's Williams who calls Thomas the best young hitter in the game today: "Thomas combines the raw strength of a Jimmie Foxx with the patience and smarts of a Tony Gwynn. He's one of the few guys I'd pay to see hit."

More Numbers

- In 1997, he became the largest man ever to win a batting title when he hit .347.
- Thomas captured the MVP two years in a row, in 1993 and 1994. In 1993, Thomas was only the tenth player in American League history to be the unanimous choice for MVP.

The Rundown

HITS: He does it all at the plate. He hits for average and he hits for power. He also has a great batting eye. He walks a lot and doesn't have a lot of strikeouts. Only Ruth and Williams have a higher on-base percentage.

OUTS: We still don't know yet what he will do over the rest of his career. No doubt his numbers have been helped by efforts to increase the offense of the game in the 1990s, especially the shrinking strike zone.

Sam Thompson, from an
early baseball card.

SAM THOMPSON

Nickname: Big Sam
Given name: Samuel Luther Thompson
Born: March 5, 1860, Danville, Indiana
Died: November 7, 1922
Size: 6'2" 207 lbs.
Bats: left
Throws: left
Position: rightfield
Career: 1885–1898, 1906

Knock runs in. That's the story in baseball. The more runs you score, the better chance you have to win. The guy who has the most RBIs, he's the guy you want on your team.

Now, the guy with the most lifetime RBIs, that's Henry Aaron. He was the best RBI man, or not? Well, he was also third in games and second in at bats. A better indication might be the number of RBIs for each game played. Who is the all-time leader in the category? You guessed it, Sam Thompson, who is just percentage points ahead of Lou Gehrig and Hank Greenberg.

So how come you never heard of the guy? Because he played almost his entire career in the nineteenth century. When it came to home runs and RBIs in those years, Sam Thompson was the man.

Thompson was a 24-year-old carpenter in Danville, Indiana, when the manager of the Detroit Wolverines of the National League came to town for an exhibition against the local team. The manager saw Thompson repairing a roof and asked him if he wanted to play. Thompson said okay, as long as he got a full day's pay. Not only did he get that, but he played so well he also got a minor league contract out of it. By the next year he was playing for the Wolverines.

When Babe Ruth hit his 129th career homer, he broke the major league lifetime record, held by . . . you guessed it again, Sam Thompson. There were years when Thompson dominated. Consider 1887, when he led the league in hitting with a .372 average, 25 points higher than Cap Anson's second-place .347 mark and 104 points higher than the league average. His RBI total that year was an astounding 166. In second place was Roger Connor's 104 followed by Anson and Dan Brouthers. All three of the men behind him were future Hall of Famers. Thompson's 166 RBIs were the highest total of the nineteenth century. Second were the 165 he had in 1895. Thompson's 166 would be the record for 34 years when it was broken by Babe Ruth.

Anson and Ed Delahanty, two great nineteenth-century swingers, had more RBIs than Thompson, but Thompson's RBIs-per-game percentages in 1895 (1.39), 1894 (1.38), and 1887 (1.31) are the three highest ever recorded.

Thompson was a big man. Like Stan Musial and Al Simmons, Thompson had an unusual batting style. He would crouch real low at the plate and then leap at the pitch, smashing line drives so hard infielders with their small gloves would duck away from them. Using that odd stance, he hit over .370 three times, including one season where he hit .404.

In the 1887 world championship series between Detroit and the Browns, Thompson became the first man to hit two homers in one postseason game. Twice he led the league in homers and in slugging. His .686 slugging average of 1894 was the third highest of the century. His runs-per-game percentage of .89 is ninth all time. He scored over 100 runs a season eight years in a row. It would have been 11 in a row, if it hadn't been for an injury that kept him out of two thirds of the 1888 season. Even so, he scored 51 runs in just 56 games. If he had been healthy, he might have scored over 140 runs.

More Numbers

• He had over 200 hits in a season three times.
• Thompson led the league in doubles twice and in singles once.
• His 23 triples in 1887 are ninth all time for a single season.

The Rundown

HITS: He might be the best RBI man in the history of the game.

OUTS: He benefited from the increased pitching distance and other rules. For example, in 1887, his best year, batters got four strikes, and walks counted as hits.

Honus Wagner.

HONUS WAGNER

Nickname: The Flying Dutchman
Given name: John Peter Wagner
Born: February 24, 1874, Chartiers,
　　　　Pennsylvania
Died: December 6, 1955
Size: 5'11" 200 lbs.
Bats: right
Throws: right
Position: shortstop
Career: 1897–1917

H onus Wagner sure didn't look like a shortstop. He wasn't long and lean, although he had long arms, long enough, people said, so that he could tie his shoes without bending his knees. The former coal miner had hands like shovels, so big people said he didn't need a glove. When he did scoop up a ball, he would often gather pebbles and dirt and send that flying along with the ball to first base. He was also stocky with a barrel chest and bowed legs that looked like a set of parentheses.

Wagner didn't hit like most shortstops either. His bat completely dominated the Dead Ball era with eight batting crowns and six slugging titles. In years when the league batting average ranged from .240 to .260, he averaged .327.

In his first three years in the league, from 1897 to 1899, he averaged .324. From 1900 to 1911, when the rest of the league's averages plummeted, he averaged .347.

It was in that stretch that he captured the batting crown eight times. That is still a National League record, although it has since been tied by Tony Gwynn. The one year between 1903 and 1909 that he didn't lead the league, he hit .363 and was outhit only by Cy Seymour's .377. Seymour somehow hit 73 points above his average that season.

To see how dominant Wagner was, let's just take 1907. That year, he hit .350. He was one of only four players to hit over .300. When Rogers Hornsby hit .424, the New York

Giants alone had seven players who topped .300. The last-place Phillies had three players over .300.

Wagner's slugging average may not rank with the leaders today, but he was the top slugger of his era, and it wasn't even close. In 1900, he led the National League with a .573 slugging average, 28 points higher than Elmer Flick's .545. In 1904, he led Mike Grady .520 to .474. In 1908, his .542 was 90 points higher than second-place Mike Donlin's.

To give you a comparison, in 1911, Cobb's best year, he led the league in slugging with a .621 average. Joe Jackson was in second at .590. In 1912, Cobb again took the slugging title with a .586 average, and again Jackson was second, but this time by only seven points.

Playing at a time when few runs were scored at all, Wagner drove in over 100 runs in a season nine times. His 126 RBIs in 1901 was the highest in the decade. Wagner also scored 100 or more runs in a season six times, a remarkable number for that period.

Like Cobb, Wagner had speed. That's why they called him "The Flying Dutchman." He didn't set the records Cobb did, but he was still the premier base thief of the Dead Ball era, leading the league five times, one behind Cobb.

Cobb and Wagner faced each other once in World Series play. In 1909, Wagner outhit Cobb .333 to .231 and he stole six bases to Cobb's two, as he led the Pirates to victory.

At one point, Cobb was on first and shouted to Wagner he was stealing on the next pitch. Most people were afraid of Cobb and his razor-sharp spikes. This time, when Cobb slid in hard, Wagner was right there to plant the ball on Cobb's face. "We know how to play hard, too," Wagner told him quietly.

When Ed Barrow was general manager of the Yankees, his star players were Babe Ruth and Lou Gehrig. He also saw Ty Cobb play at his peak, but he still rated Wagner as the best player in the history of the game. This is what he said of Wagner: "If Wagner had batted against a lively ball, he would have 50 home runs almost every year."

More Numbers

• Wagner batted .300 or over 15 consecutive years, still a National League record.
• He led the league in doubles eight times.
• His 643 doubles are eighth all time.
• He led the league in triples three times.
• His 252 lifetime triples are third all time.
• He is seventh all time in hits with 3,418.

The Rundown

HITS: Wagner dominated the Dead Ball era the way Babe Ruth dominated the 1920s. He hit for average and could also slug the ball and was one of the fastest players in the history of the game.

OUTS: Others had a higher lifetime batting average.

Ted Williams.

TED WILLIAMS

Nickname: The Splendid Splinter, The Thumper

Given name: Theodore Samuel Williams

Born: August 30, 1918

Size: 6'3" 205 lbs.

Bats: left

Throws: right

Position: leftfield

Career: 1939–1942, 1946–1960

I t was the last day of the 1941 season. The Red Sox were playing a doubleheader against the Athletics. Ted Williams was hitting .3995. Rounded up, that meant if he chose not to play he could finish the season at .400.

His manager, Joe Cronin, approached him before the first game. "Why don't you sit out the day, Ted, and have your .400."

Williams shook his head. "I don't want it that way."

So the Splendid Splinter played both ends of the double bill and was truly splendid. He went 6-for-8 to finish the season at .406, the last man to top the .400 mark.

Williams probably knew the strike zone better than any other player who ever lived. He refused to swing at pitches that were not over the plate. He even created a chart that showed how high his average would be if he swung at pitches in certain areas of the strike zone. For example, he said the highest average would be hitting pitches waist-high right over the plate; the lowest, on the bottom inside corner.

How could he be so precise? In part because he had phe-nomenal eyesight. His eyes were so sharp, he said he could follow the path of the ball from the time it left the pitcher's hand until it crossed the plate. He could even tell whether it was a fastball or a curve by watching the rotation of the seams!

Just bragging? Probably not. Williams's .208 average of walks per at bat is the highest in major league history. He led the league in walks six years in a row. Add the number of walks to his hits, and that gives him a career on-base percentage of .481, 65 points higher than Musial's, 58 points higher than Ty Cobb's, 64 points higher than Tris Speaker's. Those numbers are huge. Of the real greats, only Ruth is close with .469. Pete Rose, who holds the major league record for hits in a career, had an on-base percentage of .374.

Of all the players who hit more than 500 home runs, Williams owns the lowest strikeout ratio by far. His ratio of walks to strikeouts was nearly three to one. Babe Ruth, on the other hand, had a ratio of walks to strikeouts of 1.5 to one. Aaron's was nearly one to one.

Not only was he selective, but pitchers were afraid of him. Think about it. You're the pitcher. Here comes this great hitter, and you don't want him to beat you with an extra-base hit. What do you do? If all he gave up was a walk, the pitcher felt he got off easy. It was different with Ruth. With him, pitchers felt they had a chance of striking him out.

Here's another story that tells you how afraid opposing managers were of Williams. Lou Boudreau, who is in the Hall of Fame, was managing Cleveland. One day, when the Indians played the Red Sox, Boudreau came up with the "Ted Williams shift."

Williams was a left-handed hitter. Boudreau took his shortstop and put him in centerfield behind second base. He also moved his second baseman way over toward first base. That meant the left side of the infield was wide open for Williams. Boudreau figured he would rather have Williams hit a single than hurt him more with an extra-base hit!

And you know what? More often than not it worked. Williams had such pride, he refused to let Boudreau force him to change the way he hit by going for a single, and when other managers copied the shift, it cost Williams several hits.

Before we look at the numbers, here's something else that's important to know about his career. He lost three seasons at the peak of his career when he went into the Army during World War II. Then he lost another two seasons in 1952 and 1953 when he fought in Korea.

That's five seasons. Before his first stint in the service, he was averaging 187 hits and 32 homers a year. So you can add 935 hits and 160 homers to his career totals of 2,654 hits and 521 homers to see where he might have been in his lifetime numbers had he not gone into the service. It would give him 3,589 hits, fifth all time instead of 55th, and 681 home runs, which move him from 10th to third. So you can see how some of his career numbers are misleading.

But let's look at his amazing career. In 1939, his rookie season, Williams hit .327. He wouldn't hit that low again until 1950 when he batted .317.

He won six batting titles. In 1957, when he was 39 years old, he led the league with a .388 average. He won the title again in 1958 when he hit .328 at age 40. He would have won another in 1954 when he was 36. That year, he outhit Bobby Avila .345 to .341, but because he was walked 136 times by American League pitchers, he didn't have enough official at bats.

In 1949, he missed a third Triple Crown by the narrowest of margins when he went hitless in the last game of the season and lost the batting title to George Kell, .3429 to .3428.

Williams sure knew how to make an exit. Before the last home game of the 1960 season, Williams told his manager this would be the last game of his career. He wanted to end it all in Boston. It was a cold damp night. Williams walked in his first at bat. In his next two appearances he hit the ball hard both times, but the heavy humid air kept the ball in the stadium.

Finally, in the eighth inning, he came to the plate for the last time in his career. The crowd gave him a standing ovation as he stepped up to the plate against Jack Fisher. With the count 1-0, Fisher threw a fastball and Williams missed.

Now, Fisher stared again at the plate. He wanted to throw that heater again, and he did, but Williams was waiting for it, and he met the ball with everything he had. The ball flew out toward right center, and this time it kept going.

Williams circled the bases grinning to himself because he knew it was the perfect way to say good night to a magnificent career.

More Numbers

- Williams made the All-Star team every full year he played.
- He was twice named MVP. (He should have received the award in 1947, the year he won one of his two Triple Crowns. But a local Boston writer left him off the ballot because he just didn't like Williams. Because of that, Williams lost by one vote to DiMaggio.)
- His .406 in 1941 was the highest season average since Rogers Hornsby hit .424 in 1924.
- He led the league in various batting departments 43 times in his career. That included two Triple Crowns and four home run titles. Six times he led the league in runs scored.
- His total bases per game is 2.13, just behind Gehrig and Ruth, who were at 2.33 and 2.31.
- Williams's .634 slugging average is second to Ruth's .690.
- His .344 batting average is tied for ninth on the all-time list with Billy Hamilton and is the highest by far of the modern era.

The Rundown

HITS: Williams was the dominant hitter of the modern era by a lot. He not only hit with great power and for average but also had a fantastic batting eye.

OUTS: He had a long decline where he went over 10 years without scoring 100 runs or knocking in 100 RBIs.

WHO'S IT GONNA BE?

So there you have it. Now it's time to make your decision. Is a .366 lifetime average more important or less important than 755 lifetime homers? Is five years of excellence better than a lifetime of above-average hitting? Is it more important to get on base or to knock runners home? Would the greatest hitters of the nineteenth century be able to hit late-twentieth-century pitching? Would a power hitter of the Dead Ball era be a monster hitter today? These are things you have to decide before you choose the greatest hitter who ever lived.

Go back and weigh all the factors. Maybe come up with a few more on your own. And if you think someone should be added to the list of players we have provided, tote the numbers up on your own.

Who's it gonna be?

So, you've made your decision. Congratulations. Now try this. You know who the greatest hitter ever was over the course of an entire career. Who was the greatest hitter for one single season? Was it McGwire's 1998 with his 70 home runs? Joe DiMaggio's 1941 when he hit in 56 straight games? What about Babe Ruth's 1920 when he hit more home runs than every team but his own? Then there's George Sisler's .407 in 1920 when he established a record for hits that remains unbroken or Rogers Hornsby's 1922 season when he won the National League Triple Crown and then some.

How about the more modern players, like Mickey Mantle when he took the Triple Crown in 1956 or Jim Rice, who had over 400 total bases for the Red Sox in 1978?

Again, it's up to you. As Casey Stengel liked to say, "You can look it up."

 # FURTHER READING

Check out these great books to get your own stats and stories.

Baseball Anecdotes, by Daniel Okrent and Steve Wulf; Harper & Row; 1989. No stats here, just great stories, and lots of them, especially about the likes of Ruth, Cobb, and Gehrig.

The Baseball Encyclopedia: The Complete and Definitive Record of Major League Baseball; Macmillan. They're not kidding. Almost every important stat on every player is included here. The latest edition is the 10th, but any recent edition will give you years of great reading. The encyclopedia and the *Sporting News* were the basic sources of stats for this book.

The Glory of Their Times: The Story of the Early Days of Baseball Told by the Men Who Played It, by Lawrence Ritter; Quill; 1984. Some people say this is the best book ever written about baseball. I agree. These interviews with players, some of whom were active around the turn of the century, make for some amazing reading. You'll find plenty of stories about players included here, such as Honus Wagner, Babe Ruth, Nap Lajoie, and Joe Jackson, and an especially moving interview with Hank Greenberg.

Historical Baseball Abstract, by Bill James; Villard Books; 1988. This mathematician uses regular stats and invents a few of his own to rate the greatest players of all time. But he doesn't stop there; there's also oodles of great anecdotes and background on baseball's different eras. Much of the background on baseball's early days in this book came from here.

The Real 100 Best Baseball Players of All Time and Why!, by Ken Shouler; Addax Publishing; 1998. This includes hitters and pitchers and some more stats and arguments.

Ted Williams' Hit List, by Ted Williams and Jim Prime; Masters Press; 1996. The Splendid Splinter was not only great with the bat, but also with his opinions about who he thinks are the greatest hitters of all times. Includes lots of stats to back up his arguments. Most of Williams's comments about other hitters that I quote here came from his *Hit List.*

Voices from Cooperstown: Baseball Hall of Famers Tell It Like It Was, by Anthony J. Connor; Galahad Books; 1998. No stats here, just great stories from the Hall of Famers themselves.

Hitting Statistics (Career)

Player	Avg.	Games	At Bats	Hits	HR	RBI	SLG	Runs	2B	3B	BB	K
Aaron, Hank	.305	3298	12364	3771	755	2297	.555	2174	624	98	1402	1383
Bonds, Barry												
Brouthers, Dan	.342	1673	6711	2296	106	1296	.519	1523	460	205	840	238
Burkett, Jesse	.338	2066	8421	2850	75	952	.446	1720	320	182	1029	230
Clemente, Roberto	.317	2433	9454	3000	240	1305	.475	1416	440	166	621	1230
Cobb, Ty	.366	3035	11434	4189	117	1937	.512	2246	724	295	1249	357
Delahanty, Ed	.346	1835	7505	2596	101	1464	.505	1599	522	185	741	244
DiMaggio, Joe	.325	1736	6821	2214	361	1537	.579	1390	389	131	790	369
Foxx, Jimmie	.325	2317	8134	2646	534	1922	.609	1751	458	125	1452	1311
Gehrig, Lou	.340	2164	8001	2721	493	1995	.632	1888	534	163	1508	790
Greenberg, Hank	.313	1394	5193	1628	331	1276	.605	1051	379	71	852	844
Griffey, Ken, Jr.												
Gwynn, Tony												
Heilmann, Harry	.342	2148	7787	2660	183	1539	.520	1291	542	151	856	550
Hornsby, Rogers	.358	2259	8173	2930	301	1584	.577	1579	541	169	1038	679
Jackson, Joe	.356	1332	4981	1772	54	785	.517	873	307	168	519	158
Keeler, Willie	.341	2123	8591	2932	33	810	.415	1719	241	145	524	36
Lajoie, Nap	.338	2480	9589	3242	83	1599	.467	1504	657	163	516	85
Lombardi, Ernie	.306	1853	5855	1792	190	990	.460	601	277	27	430	262

Player	Avg.	Games	At Bats	Hits	HR	RBI	SLG	Runs	2B	3B	BB	K
Mantle, Mickey	.298	2401	8102	2415	536	1509	.557	1677	344	72	1733	1710
Mays, Willie	.302	2992	10881	3283	660	1903	.557	2062	523	140	1464	1526
McGwire, Mark												
Musial, Stan	.331	3026	10972	3630	475	1951	.559	1949	725	177	1599	696
Ruth, Babe	.342	2503	8399	2873	714	2213	.690	2174	506	136	2056	1330
Simmons, Al	.334	2215	8759	2927	307	1827	.535	1507	539	149	615	737
Sisler, George	.340	2055	8267	2812	102	1175	.468	1284	425	164	472	327
Speaker, Tris	.345	2789	10195	3514	117	1529	.500	1882	792	222	1381	220
Terry, Bill	.341	1721	6428	2193	154	1078	.506	1120	373	112	537	449
Thomas, Frank												
Thompson, Sam	.331	1407	5984	1979	127	1299	.505	1256	340	160	450	226
Wagner, Honus	.327	2792	10430	3415	101	1732	.466	1736	640	252	963	327
Williams, Ted	.344	2292	7706	2654	521	1839	.634	1798	525	71	2019	709

INDEX

(Page numbers in **boldface** refer to profiles of specific hitters. Page numbers in *italic* refer to Hitting Statistics chart.)